MICROSOFT
EXCEL
BASICS

This is a **FLAME TREE** book
First published 2015

Publisher and Creative Director: Nick Wells
Project Editor: Catherine Taylor
Art Director and Layout Design: Mike Spender
Digital Design and Production: Chris Herbert
Copy Editor: Anna Groves
Screenshots: Roger Laing
Original Text: Rob Hawkins
Proofreader: Dawn Laker
Indexer: Helen Snaith

Special thanks to: Monique Jensen

This edition first published 2015 by
FLAME TREE PUBLISHING
Crabtree Hall, Crabtree Lane
Fulham, London SW6 6TY
United Kingdom

www.flametreepublishing.com

EVERYDAY GUIDES MADE EASY

MICROSOFT EXCEL BASICS

ROGER LAING

SERIES FOREWORD BY MARK MAYNE

FLAME TREE
PUBLISHING

CONTENTS

Find out what all that spreadsheet jargon means and follow our
no-nonsense instructions on using workbooks.

Discover quick techniques for working with cells as well as entering, deleting and editing data.

Excel's tools for dealing with large amounts of data – from freezing panes and multiple views
to subtotals and PivotTables.

The best techniques and step-by-step guides to running calculations, creating charts and
printing out your spreadsheets.

How to avoid some common problems in Excel and resolve them if they do occur.

Using mobile apps or Excel Online to create and edit your spreadsheets.

SERIES FOREWORD

Windows, launched in 1985, began as a way to navigate PCs without having to resort to command prompts, and, although early versions might look clunky by today's standards, the concept of navigating a computer through 'windows' rather than through hard-to-remember commands immediately caught on. Millions of installs later, Windows is the most popular computer operating system on the planet, with more than 1.25 billion PCs running a version of Windows today.

To complement Windows in the business space, Microsoft developed Microsoft Office back in 1990, and without Office programs like Word, Excel and Powerpoint our world would look very different today.

This guide on Microsoft Excel is designed to take you from zero to hero without any of the pain, but fear not, we won't bamboozle you with jargon. We'll mainly cover the basics of this feature-rich software, progressing through to some advanced functions and finally troubleshooting and mobile Excel. Each chapter has a number of Hot Tips that'll ensure you're on the very cutting edge without lifting a finger.

This step-by-step guide is written by an acknowledged expert on Excel, so you can be sure of the best advice, and is suitable for anyone from the complete beginner through to slightly more advanced users who would like a refresher. You'll find this guide an excellent reference volume on Excel, and it will grace your bookcase for years to come.

Mark Mayne
Editor of T3.com

INTRODUCTION

Microsoft Excel first appeared in 1985. Since then, this computerized spreadsheet has evolved, with an increasing number of features that can be very confusing for the beginner. This book will help you get started and rapidly build your skills.

NEED TO KNOW

Filled with practical advice, *Microsoft Excel Basics* will guide you through the essentials of using Excel, as well as some of the more advanced features – such as creating charts or PivotTables – to help you become more proficient.

SMALL CHUNKS

Every chapter has short paragraphs describing particular features within Excel and how to use them. They don't have to be read in order, just dip into individual sections as needed.

STEP-BY-STEP GUIDES

These provide clear and concise instructions on using Excel for a variety of tasks, from summarizing expenses to creating a travel mileage guide to your favourite locations.

SIX CHAPTERS

This book is split into six chapters. The first explains the jargon used in Excel and gets you started using workbooks. The second covers quick and easy techniques for working with cells, as well as entering, formatting and editing your information. Chapter three has useful time-savers for dealing with large amounts of data. Chapter four covers some of the more advanced features in Excel, such as calculations in Word and creating charts as well as printing out your spreadsheets. Chapter five looks at some common problems in Excel and how to resolve them. Finally, in chapter six, discover the mobile apps available for tablets and smartphones and see how you can use Excel Online from any computer.

Above: Excel comes with a set of templates you can easily adapt to carry out everyday tasks.

Hot Tips

Look out for the Hot Tips, which tell you about the many shortcuts and quick techniques available in Excel.

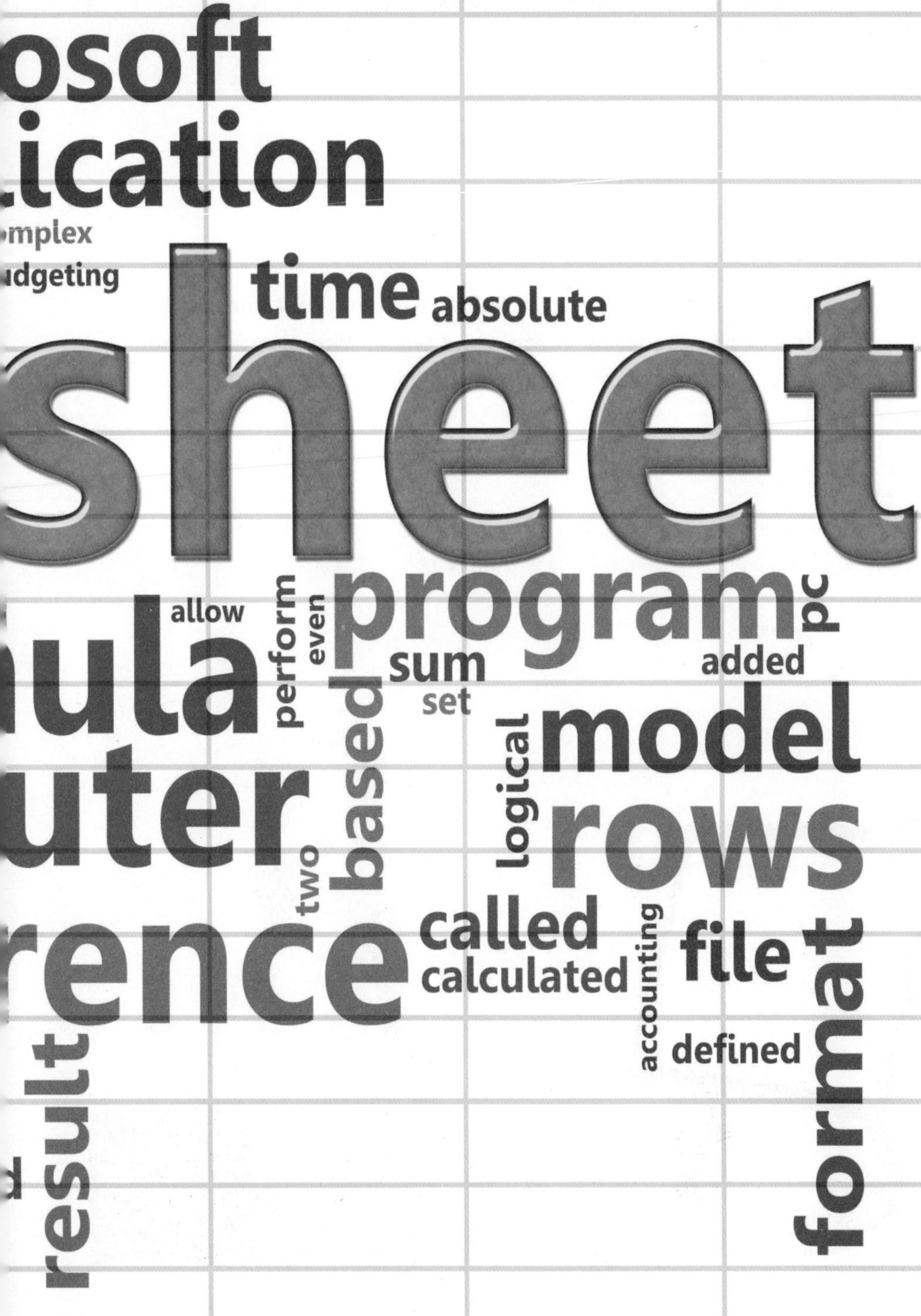

osoft
ication
mplex
udgeting

time absolute

sheet

allow perform even **program** pc

ula

sum

added

uter

set

model

two based logical **rows**

rence

called accounting **file**

calculated

result

defined

format

EXCEL JARGON

Excel can seem more confusing than it really is if you don't know the meaning of some of the technical terms used within the program. This section provides a quick reference guide to Excel's jargon.

SPREADSHEET

A spreadsheet is quite literally a method of spreading information across a sheet. A computer spreadsheet resembles a piece of paper with a grid printed on it.

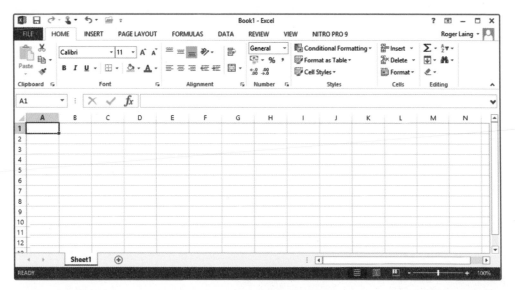

Above: A spreadsheet, more properly known as a worksheet, with its familiar grid format.

Worksheets

Programs such as Excel are referred to as spreadsheet programs, and the files they create are known as spreadsheets. Many people call a single page or sheet in a file a spreadsheet, although these are properly known as worksheets.

ROWS

The lines or cells *across* a spreadsheet are known as rows. Each row is identified by a row number, which is displayed down the left-hand side of the screen.

Ever-Increasing Numbers

Excel currently supports over a million (1,048,576) rows! This might appear excessive, but in fact they can be easily filled.

Hot Tip

Have trouble remembering which are rows and which are columns? In a rowing boat, you row across the water – just as the rows in Excel are across the page.

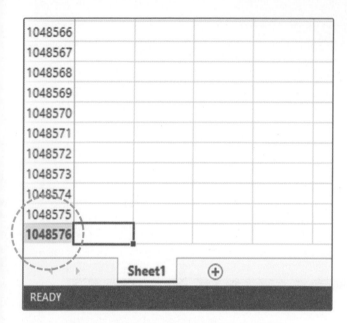

Above: Excel has more than a million rows in each worksheet.

COLUMNS

The cells *down* a spreadsheet are called columns and are identified by a series of alphabetically ordered letters across the top of the worksheet. They run from A to Z, then AA, AB, AC to AZ, followed by BA, BB, BC, and so on. Excel currently supports 16,384 columns in a single worksheet.

CELLS

A particular point in the grid of a spreadsheet is referred to as a cell. The location is identified by a cell reference, for example A10 refers to column A and row 10.

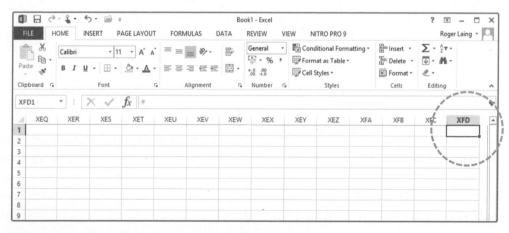

Above: Even though there are 16,384 columns in each Excel worksheet, it is possible to fill them.

Hot Tip

You can have as many worksheets in a workbook as you like. The only limit is the amount of memory available to run them.

WORKBOOK

This is the name for an Excel file that contains one or more spreadsheet pages (worksheets). The terms 'file' and 'workbook' are interchangeable. Each workbook opens in its own window to make it easy to work on two at the same time.

WORKSHEET

A single page of an Excel spreadsheet is known as a worksheet. Each worksheet is displayed as one of a series of tabs near the bottom left of the active page, like the pages of a book.

RIBBON

Excel has a Ribbon instead of the traditional drop-down menus and buttons. Above the Ribbon is a series of tabs. Click a tab, such as View, and groups of buttons related to it – like Workbook Views – appear on the Ribbon below.

Hot Tip

Minimize or maximize the Ribbon by pressing Ctrl on the keyboard, then F1.

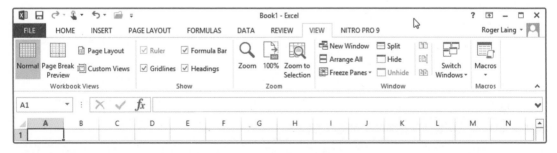

Above: The Ribbon groups together various Excel commands that have similar functions. To access different ones, click the various tabs above the Ribbon.

USES FOR EXCEL

Excel has evolved from being a specialist calculations-based program, used mainly by accountants and statisticians, to offering a wide variety of functions that almost everyone will find useful. Here you will find some examples of how Excel can be used.

ORGANIZE YOUR LIFE

The range of projects you can do in Excel is amazing:

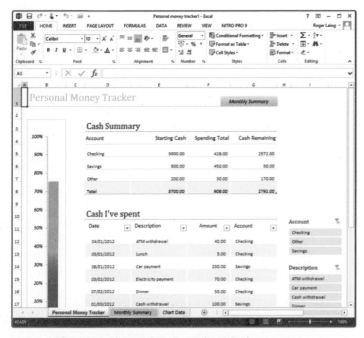

Above: Among the many things you can do with Excel is set up your own money tracker.

- Download bank and credit card **statements**.

- Set up expenses and mileage claim **forms**.

- **Track** your personal finances.

- Keep a **running total** of your valuables.

- Track your **warranties**.

- **Compare prices** for everything from holidays to cars.

- Set up prioritized **to-do lists**.

EXCEL VERSIONS

The current version of the program is Excel 2013, which is available by subscription for the PC (Excel 2011 for the Mac). It is part of Office 365, which includes other Microsoft programs, including Word (a word-processing program) and Outlook (for emails).

EXCEL ONLINE OPTIONS

There are various subscriptions plans available for Office Online. Whichever you choose, it will include Excel, as it's one of the core Office programs.

Online Subscriptions

- **Office 365 Personal:** Lets you install Excel and the other programs on a single computer and one tablet for a monthly or annual subscription.

- **Office 365 Home:** Your subscription lets you install Excel and the other programs on up to five desktops or laptops (PC and Mac). In addition, you can install it on up to five tablets, such as the Apple iPad or Microsoft Surface.

Above: All the online subscriptions to Office include access to Excel.

Above: Access your Excel files from anywhere on OneDrive, which gives you 15 GB of free storage.

○ **Office 365 for Business:** Includes Microsoft Excel, plus a wider range of business applications.

STANDALONE VERSIONS

There are also desktop versions of Excel (where you pay a one-off fee for the program). Excel 2013 is the latest for the PC, Excel 2011 for the Mac.

LINKED BY THE CLOUD

You can work on your latest Excel spreadsheet anywhere, thanks to special versions of the program being available for your PC, tablet and smartphone and at Office Online. To keep them up to date, Excel lets you save and share your files via the cloud – or more precisely, OneDrive. This is free online storage space from where you can sync your files to any of your devices. You can sign up for your OneDrive account at www.onedrive.com.

EXCEL ON THE MACINTOSH

Excel on the Apple
Macintosh works in much the same
way as it does on a Windows platform.
Both versions have a similar look and feel and have the
same features, which makes it easy to share files between PCs and
Macs. Although this book uses Excel for the PC for examples, most of
the information applies equally to the Apple Mac.

A Note on Keyboard Differences

The keyboard-related instructions in this book are for PCs. However, as keyboards vary wildly,
yours may not have the same keys or work in the same way. In particular, the keys on Apple
Macs are different. For example, the equivalent of the PC Ctrl key on the Apple Mac is the
Command (⌘/⌘) key (not the one labelled 'Ctrl', confusingly!). Page Up/Down keys are only
available on full-size Apple Mac keyboards – marked as arrows with two short horizontal lines.
However, you can get the same result by pressing the Fn key and up or down arrow. With an
older mouse, to right-click on an Apple Mac, press Ctrl + click.

ON THE SCREEN

The main screen in Excel can seem bewildering if you don't know what you're looking for. The following pages provide detailed explanations of what's there.

EXCEL ON PCS

The tabbed Ribbon system means the Excel screen looks very different to early versions.

It is context-sensitive, which means that when you click a tab, the available options change.

1 **Title bar:** The title bar appears at the top of all Microsoft applications. It displays the name of the application and the current workbook.

2 **Quick Access Toolbar:** Usually displayed at the top-left corner of the screen, it has some buttons for 'commands' (tasks) you commonly use, such as Open, Save, Undo and Print.

Above: The Quick Access Toolbar has some of the tasks you frequently use, like Save or Open a file.

3 **Minimize button:** This reduces the Excel window and displays it as a button on the Windows taskbar.

4 **Maximize/Restore button:** If there's a single box, then clicking on it will enlarge the Excel page to fill the screen (maximize). If there are two boxes (restore), then clicking the button will reduce the Excel window.

Above: Although Excel can seem confusing, you'll soon find your way round its many features.

⑤ **Close button:** The close button on the title bar will shut Excel.

⑥ **Ribbon tabs:** These are labelled File, Home, Insert, Page Layout, Formulas, Data, Review and View.

⑦ **Ribbon:** Clicking on each tab changes the buttons on the Ribbon, which are grouped into similar tasks, such as Calculation on the Formulas tab.

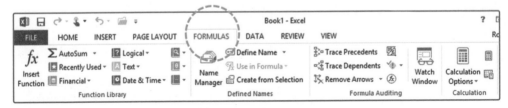

Above: Each tab groups similar commands or tasks together on the Ribbon, like Calculation here on the Formulas tab.

⑧ **Name box:** This has the cell address, or name, of the currently selected cell.

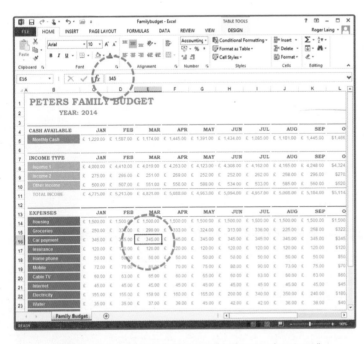

Above: When you select a cell, a thick green box shows it is the active cell. The cell's contents also show in the Formula bar.

⑨ **Formula bar:** Displays the contents of the selected cell.

⑩ **Select-all button:** Click this and the entire worksheet is selected.

⑪ **Column headings:** The column headings display the column labels from A to Z, then AA to AZ, BA to BZ, and so on.

⑫ **Active cell indicator:** A dark border identifies the cell or group of cells selected.

13 **Row headings**: Displays the row numbers in a spreadsheet.

14 **Vertical scroll bar**: This allows you to scroll up and down through the worksheet.

15 **Tab scroll buttons**: These are used to scroll through the worksheet tabs if they are not visible. Right-click on any of these buttons for a list of worksheets.

16 **Sheet tabs**: The sheet tabs display the names of the worksheets in the workbook. Click on a sheet's tab to make it active.

17 **Insert worksheet**: Click the + button to the right of the sheet tabs to add a new worksheet.

18 **Horizontal scroll bar**: The horizontal scroll bar allows you to scroll left and right through the columns of the worksheet.

19 **Resize the horizontal scroll bar**: The three vertical dots button to the left of the

Hot Tip

You can split the window vertically or horizontally to view two areas of the document at the same time. Highlight the row or column where you want the divide, select the View tab and press the Split button.

	INCOME TYPE	JAN	FEB	MAR	APR	
6						
7	INCOME TYPE	JAN	FEB	MAR	APR	
8	Income 1	£ 4,000.00	£ 4,410.00	£ 4,019.00	£ 4,263.00	£ 4,
9	Income 2	£ 275.00	£ 296.00	£ 251.00	£ 269.00	£
10	Other Income	£ 500.00	£ 507.00	£ 551.00	£ 556.00	£
11	TOTAL INCOME	£ 4,775.00	£ 5,213.00	£ 4,821.00	£ 5,088.00	£ 4,
12						
13	EXPENSES	JAN	FEB	MAR	APR	
14	Housing	£ 1,500.00	£ 1,500.00	£ 1,500.00	£ 1,500.00	£ 1,
15	Groceries	£ 250.00	£ 331.00	£ 299.00	£ 333.00	£
16	Car payment	£ 345.00	£ 345.00	£ 345.00	£ 345.00	£
17	Insurance	£ 120.00	£ 120.00	£ 120.00	£ 120.00	£
18	Home phone	£ 50.00	£ 50.00	£ 50.00	£ 50.00	£
19	Mobile	£ 72.00	£ 70.00	£ 80.00	£ 70.00	£
20	Cable TV	£ 60.00	£ 63.00	£ 65.00	£ 60.00	£
21	Internet	£ 45.00	£ 45.00	£ 45.00	£ 45.00	£
22	Electricity	£ 155.00	£ 155.00	£ 158.00	£ 160.00	£
23	Water	£ 35.00	£ 35.00	£ 37.00	£ 39.00	£

Family Budget   ⊕

READY   New sheet

Above: Click the + sign to open a new, blank worksheet.

horizontal scroll bar lets you resize it. Position the mouse pointer over it and, when it changes to a cross with two arrows, drag the mouse left or right.

20 **Status bar**: The left side of the Status bar displays the current command or operation.

21 **Zoom control**: Drag the slider to zoom in and out or click the percentage value to change.

22 **Layouts**: Click on the small buttons to change between views – Normal, Page Layout and Page Break Preview.

		JAN	FEB	MAR	APR	MAY	JUN	JUI
YEAR: 2014								
CASH AVAILABLE		JAN	FEB	MAR	APR	MAY	JUN	JUI
Monthly Cash	£	1,220.00	£ 1,587.00	£ 1,174.00	£ 1,445.00	£ 1,391.00	£ 1,434.00	£ 1,085.00
INCOME TYPE		JAN	FEB	MAR	APR	MAY	JUN	JUI
Income 1	£	4,000.00	£ 4,410.00	£ 4,019.00	£ 4,263.00	£ 4,123.00	£ 4,308.00	£ 4,162.00
Income 2	£	275.00	£ 296.00	£ 251.00	£ 269.00	£ 252.00	£ 252.00	£ 262.00
Other Income	£	500.00	£ 507.00	£ 551.00	£ 556.00	£ 588.00	£ 534.00	£ 533.00
TOTAL INCOME	£	4,775.00	£ 5,213.00	£ 4,821.00	£ 5,088.00	£ 4,963.00	£ 5,094.00	£ 4,957.00
EXPENSES		JAN	FEB	MAR	APR	MAY	JUN	JUI
Housing	£	1,500.00	£ 1,500.00	£ 1,500.00	£ 1,500.00	£ 1,500.00	£ 1,500.00	£ 1,500.00
Groceries	£	250.00	£ 331.00	£ 299.00	£ 333.00	£ 324.00	£ 313.00	£ 338.00
Car payment	£	345.00	£ 345.00	£ 345.00	£ 345.00	£ 345.00	£ 345.00	£ 345.00
Insurance	£	120.00	£ 120.00	£ 120.00	£ 120.00	£ 120.00	£ 120.00	£ 120.00
Home phone	£	50.00	£ 50.00	£ 50.00	£ 50.00	£ 50.00	£ 50.00	£ 50.00
Mobile	£	72.00	£ 70.00	£ 80.00	£ 70.00	£ 75.00	£ 80.00	£ 90.00
Cable TV	£	60.00	£ 63.00	£ 65.00	£ 60.00	£ 65.00	£ 60.00	£ 63.00
Internet	£	45.00	£ 45.00	£ 45.00	£ 45.00	£ 45.00	£ 45.00	£ 45.00

Family Budget

READY   PAGE: 1 OF 1   100%

Above: Use the Layouts buttons on the Status bar to change the view of your spreadsheet. This does the same as clicking the Workbook Views buttons on the Ribbon, under the View tab.

EXCEL ON MACS

As you can see from the screenshot below, the layout of Excel on Apple Macs is very similar to that on PCs. Most of the numbered descriptions on pages 18–22 apply here, with only a few minor differences; for example, the zoom control is on the top toolbar.

Hot Tip

When using the zoom control, you can click on the plus (+) and minus (–) symbols as well as dragging the slider to zoom in and out or clicking on the percentage value to change the figure manually.

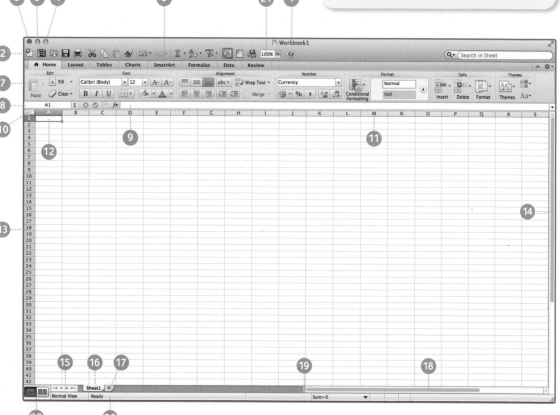

Above: Although Excel can seem confusing you'll soon find your way round its many features.

GETTING STARTED IN EXCEL

Now that you are familiar with what's onscreen in Excel, it's time to get to grips with some basic functions, such as opening, closing and saving Excel files, and making sure files are not lost.

OPENING AND CLOSING EXCEL

There are several ways of opening Excel, so it's worth trying them all to see which is fastest and easiest for you.

Opening Excel

○ **Windows 8.1**: On the Windows 8.1 Start screen, double-click the icon for Excel 2013. To open it in traditional Desktop mode, right-click the Excel 2013 icon on the Start screen and select Pin to Taskbar.

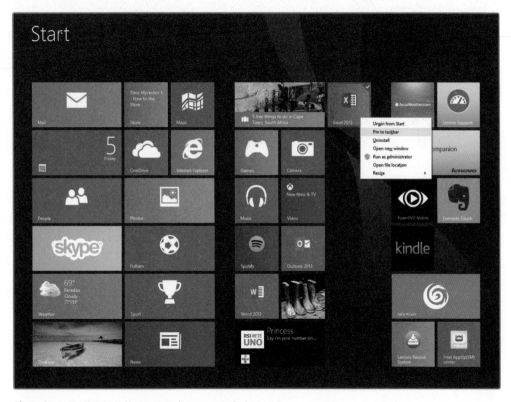

Above: Pinning Excel to the taskbar means it always opens in Desktop mode.

○ **Taskbar**: Once pinned to the taskbar, you'll see Excel's green icon. Click this to open the program.

○ **Open an Excel file**: Opening an Excel file will automatically open the program. Excel files are usually stored in your Documents folder.

Above: Some keyboards have an Excel symbol displayed on one of the function keys – a quick way of opening the program.

○ **Keyboard shortcut:** Some keyboards have an Excel symbol on one of the Function keys (for example, F3), which opens Excel. You may have to hold down another key to activate it.

Closing Excel

○ **File menu:** Click the File tab and select Close from the left-hand menu that appears. If any Excel files have not been saved, you will be prompted to save them before the program closes.

○ **File menu using the keyboard:** Hold down the Alt key on the keyboard, then press F followed by C for Close.

○ **Close button:** Click the X button in the top-right corner of the Excel window. If other Excel windows are open, only that file will close, otherwise the program will shut down.

○ **Keyboard shortcut:** Hold down Alt + F4 key.

- **Right-click the Excel icon on the taskbar**: Select Close window (or Close all windows if several files are open) from the pop-up menu.

OPENING NEW AND OLD EXCEL FILES

Excel workbooks or files can be opened and created in a variety of ways:

Creating a New Blank Excel File

- **Keyboard**: Press the Ctrl and N keys together.

- **Ribbon**: Click the File tab and choose New from the menu on the left. From the templates that appear, select Blank workbook to open a new file.

Opening and Saving in Backstage View

While the Ribbon has all the commands for working with your spreadsheet, press the File tab and you enter Backstage View.

This has all the commands necessary to do things to your files, such as Save, Save As, Open, Print and so on. If you are familiar with the traditional Windows Open or Save As dialogue boxes, you can go back to them. Click the File tab and select Options, then Save. Check the box beside Don't show the Backstage when opening or saving files. The change will apply to all your Office programs, not just Excel.

Above: Select Blank workbook to open a new Excel file.

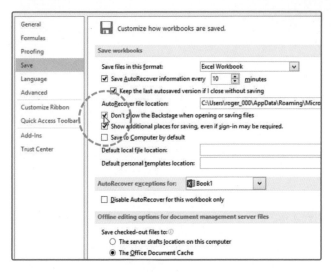

Above: If you turn off Backstage for opening or saving files, it will apply to all Office programs, including Excel.

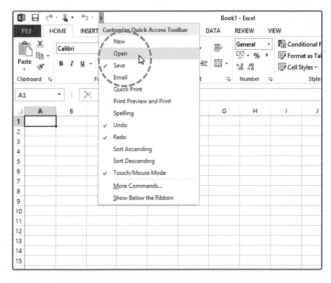

Above: It's easy to add a button to the Quick Access Toolbar to open files.

Opening a Recently Used Excel File

○ **Ribbon:** Click the File tab, then Open, to see a list of the most recent Excel files. Click on one to open it.

○ **Taskbar:** With Excel open, right-click its icon on the taskbar. In the pop-up window that appears, click any of the recent files to open them.

Opening an Old Excel File

You can use the Open window to locate an Excel file and open it:

○ **Keyboard shortcut:** Hold down the Ctrl key and letter O (not the zero). From the Open window, select where you want to look for the workbook and click the file to open it.

○ **Ribbon:** Click the File tab and choose Open.

○ **Quick Access Toolbar:** If there's a yellow-coloured folder at the top of the Excel window, click it to access the Open page. If there is no toolbar button, click the drop-down button beside the Quick Access Toolbar and choose Open from the menu that appears.

Using Windows File Explorer to Open Excel Files

Open Windows File Explorer in Desktop mode and click on Documents. Any Excel file can be opened from here without starting the program first.

SAVING FILES

It is good practice to save your Excel files regularly, but if a computer problem occurs, there are some recovery methods to ensure all is not lost.

Saving an Excel Workbook for the First Time

If you are working in a new Excel file that hasn't been previously saved, then you will need to name and save it. The quickest way to do this is to press Ctrl + S. On the Save As page, in Backstage View, choose the place where you want to store it.

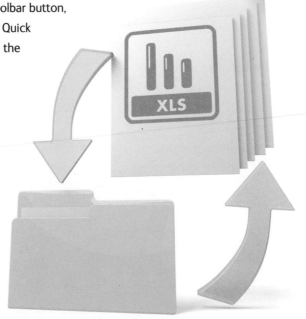
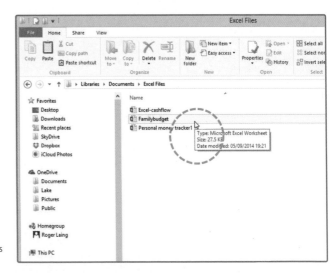

Right: Use Windows File Explorer to access your Excel files and open them, without starting the Excel program first.

Then, in the Save As dialogue box, locate the folder in which you want to store it, add a filename and click the Save button.

Resaving Excel Files

While working on a workbook, it's a good idea to save the file every few minutes to avoid losing data if a computer problem occurs:

- **Keyboard shortcut**: Press Ctrl + S. You won't see much happening (possibly a brief message on the status bar), but the file will have been saved.

- **Toolbar button**: Click on the Save button, which looks like a floppy disk, on the Quick Access Toolbar. The word Save will appear if you hover over it.

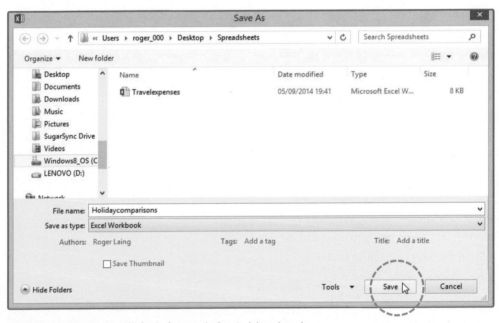

Above: As part of saving an Excel file for the first time, the Save As dialogue box asks you to name the file and choose a location in which to store it.

- **Autosave**: Excel will take the strain and save your file regularly. The saved information is then used for AutoRecover should your computer crash. To set how often Excel saves your work, go to the File tab, select Options from the left-hand menu, then Save. Here, you can change the time interval between saves and the default location.

Changing Filenames

To change the name of an Excel file, or save a copy of it with a different name, without overwriting the old file:

Hot Tip

Filenames can be quickly renamed within your Documents Library. Just select a file, press F2 on the keyboard and type a new name for the file.

- **Open** the file you want to rename.

- Press **F12** on the keyboard.

- Enter a new filename in the **Save As** dialogue box.

- Choose a different **storage location** if required.

- Click **Save**.

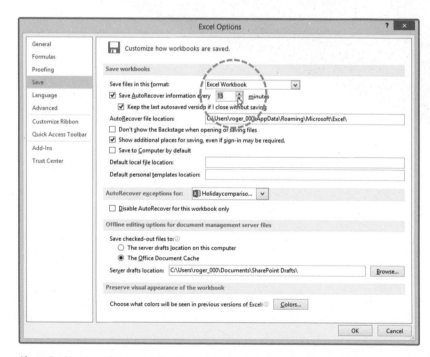

Above: Excel automatically saves your files; here, you can change the time interval between saves.

BASIC RULES OF DATA ENTRY

Entering data into an Excel spreadsheet may seem straightforward, but there are some easy mistakes to avoid.

PRESS ENTER

When typing data into a cell, press Enter/Return on the keyboard when you have finished rather than just moving to the next cell, as this can lead to mistakes, especially in calculations.

Tick and Cross

As you enter words or numbers into a cell, the tick and cross next to the Formula bar are highlighted:

- **Click on the tick**: To confirm completion, instead of pressing the Enter/Return key on the keyboard.

- **Click on the cross mark**: To go back to the cell's original contents. This is similar to using the Undo button.

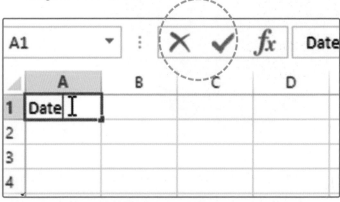

Above: When entering data into a cell, the cross and tick marks beside the Formula bar are highlighted.

Hot Tip

Press Escape on the keyboard to cancel editing a cell or entering data into it.

DATA ENTRY SHORTCUTS

Entering data can become a mind- (and finger-) numbing task, especially if you have long lists of figures to input. Excel offers a number of shortcuts to speed up the process.

AUTOCOMPLETE

Excel automatically helps you enter lists. It looks at the cells above the active one and assumes that entries will be repeated. So, if you are listing your household expenses, you won't have to type them out in full. Excel will predict what you're typing based on the first letter and you can select from the list of options it provides by pressing Enter.

C4 ▼ ⋮	✕ ✓ *fx*	Supermarket			
	A	B	C	D	E	F
1	Date	Amount	Type of Expense			
2	03-Sep	£88.00	Supermarket			
3	08-Sep	£56.40	Petrol			
4	09-Sep	£102.00	Supermarket			
5						

Above: Excel offers suggestions when entering data in a list, based on the entries above the active cell.

Understanding AutoComplete

○ **Entries starting with the same letter:** If there are several (for example, 'gas bill' and 'groceries'), Excel will wait until you enter more letters before offering AutoComplete suggestions. For example, only once you type 'gr' will Excel display 'groceries'.

○ **Continuous list**: If there are any blank cells in a list, Excel will not check the entries above it.

○ **Capital letters**: If a word in a list begins with a capital letter, AutoComplete will automatically follow the same formatting.

○ **To ignore an AutoComplete entry**: Either continue typing to overwrite it or press the delete key.

Hot Tip

Press Ctrl and the letter D to enter the contents of the cell above (provided it has data in it) into a selected cell.

◢	A	B	C	D	E	F	G
2	03-Jul	Tesco Store Brooklands	-87.5	3608.56			
3	04-Jul	Shanti Indian Restaurant	-37.9	3646.46			
4	05-Jul	Esso Coronation SSTN	-64.98	3711.44			
5	06-Jul	Bowling Green Inn	-23	3734.44			
6	06-Jul	RAC Motoring Services	-109	3843.44			
7	06-Jul	Odeon Cinemas	-42	3885.44			
8	07-Jul	Tiffin's	-6.78	3892.22			
9							
10		Bowling Green Inn					
11		Esso Coronation SSTN Odeon Cinemas					
12		RAC Motoring Services					
13		Shanti Indian Restaurant Tesco Store Brooklands					
14		Tiffin's					
15							
16							
17							
18							
19							
20							

Above: When entering a long list, press Alt + the down arrow to get a drop-down list of suggestions based on previous entries.

ALT + DOWN

Another way to speed up entering a list is to select the last entry, then press Alt and the down arrow. A pop-up menu lists all the entries so far. Left-click to select the entry you want.

Uses for Alt + Down

Although not as quick as using AutoComplete, Alt + Down is a useful way of checking for mistakes in a list and reduces the risk of entering the same listing with different spellings.

AUTOFILL

This is used when you want to add the same data, or a sequence of data (such as days of the week or months), to a block of cells.

Step-by-Step: AutoFill Months

To enter the months of the year into a spreadsheet:

1.   Type the **first month** in a cell.

2.   Press **Enter** on the keyboard.

> ## Hot Tip
>
> AutoFill is useful for creating a sequence of names with numbers. For example, if you need a list of weeks starting at Week 1, Week 2, Week 3, just enter Week 1 in a cell and use AutoFill to complete the sequence.

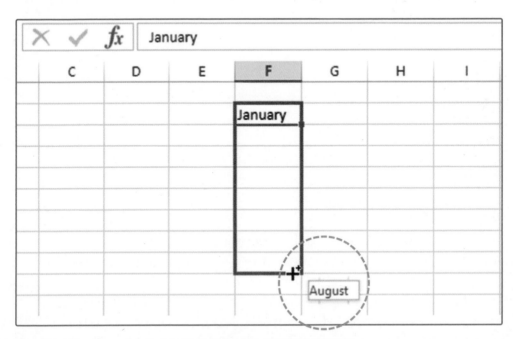

Above: To create a sequence of months, just enter the first one and use AutoFill to add the rest.

3. **Select** the cell and hover the **mouse** over the bottom-right corner of that cell.

4. When the mouse pointer changes to a **black cross**, hold the **left button** down on the mouse and move up, down or across the screen to create a sequence of months.

5. Release the **left button** on the mouse to enter the sequence.

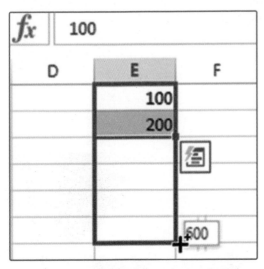

Above: To AutoFill a sequence, select two cells together, and make sure the mouse pointer changes to a black cross.

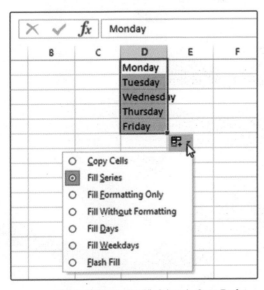

Above: After using AutoFill, click on the Smart Tag for more Fill or formatting options.

Copying with AutoFill

Calculations, titles and numbers can all be quickly copied up, down or across a spreadsheet using AutoFill. Just select the cell you want to copy and use the technique described above. If the cells to be copied are in a table, double-click on the AutoFill cross instead of dragging it.

AutoFill Number Sequences

To AutoFill a specific sequence of numbers or dates – such as 100, 200, 300 – Excel needs to know what sequence you want.

1.   Enter the **first two numbers** into adjacent cells.

2.   **Select** the two cells together (hover the mouse pointer, which should be a white cross, over the first cell, left-click and then select the second cell).

3.   Position the mouse pointer at the bottom-right corner of the selected cells (it will change to a **black cross**) and AutoFill.

AutoFill Smart Tags

After using Excel's AutoFill feature to copy data or create a sequence, a small Smart Tag will appear at the bottom of the range of cells. Click on the Smart Tag to open a menu offering more AutoFill options, including Copy Cells, Fill Formatting Only and Fill Series.

COPYING, PASTING, MOVING, DELETING AND EDITING

By copying and rearranging existing data, you can avoid hours of repetitive typing. Excel offers a variety of options to save time.

SELECTING CELLS

Below are some of the most common methods of selecting and moving cells within a worksheet.

Swipe with the Mouse

The most popular way is to hold your mouse pointer over a cell, left-click and, making sure the pointer has changed to a white cross, swipe over the block of cells you want.

Shift and Arrow Keys

The arrow keys move the cell selector around the spreadsheet. Press the Shift key and arrow keys to select the cells you want.

Ctrl, Shift and Arrow Keys

This is the ideal method for selecting large lists:

	A
1	Monday
2	Tuesday
3	Wednesday
4	Thursday
5	Friday
6	

- **Select** the cell(s) at the top of the list.

- Hold down the **Ctrl** and **Shift** keys.

- Press the **down arrow** once so the cell selector jumps to the bottom of the list or first empty space.

Above: When swiping over and selecting cells using the mouse with the left button held down, always make sure the mouse pointer is a large white cross before starting.

- **Repeat** this process if you need to move further down.

- All the cells from the top of the list to the first empty cell will be selected.

Hot Tip

If you want to select across rather than down a list, use the same instructions as above, but use the right arrow instead of the down arrow.

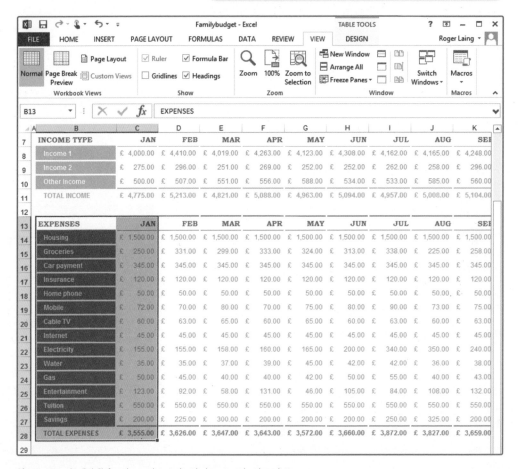

Above: Using the Ctrl, Shift and arrow keys is the ideal way to select large lists.

Ctrl, Shift and Space Bar

An entire list or table of data can be instantly selected (provided there are no blank columns or rows) by going to one cell inside the list, holding down the Ctrl and Shift keys and pressing the space bar once.

Shift and Click

This is a safe, easy way to highlight a range of cells. Click the cell in the top-left corner and scroll down to the bottom-right corner.

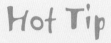

Hot Tip

Tidy up your data before selecting it by deleting unwanted rows or columns.

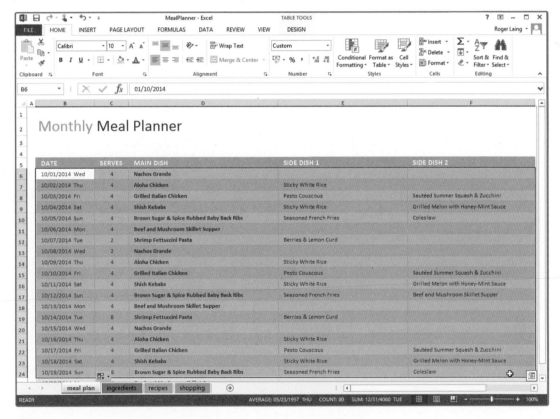

Above: The Shift and click method is one of the quickest ways of selecting a large group of cells.

Position the mouse pointer over that cell and hold down the Shift key *before* left-clicking once.

Ctrl and Click
Hold down the Ctrl key and left-click inside individual cells, or as you swipe over a range of cells, to select them.

CUT, COPY AND PASTE TECHNIQUES
Use these commands to move, remove and duplicate information:

Keyboard Shortcuts
- **Cut**: To clear information from cells, select them and press the Delete key. To cut content ready to paste, press Ctrl + X.

- **Copy**: Press Ctrl + C. Excel adds a moving dotted line around the selected cell or cells. Select the cell(s) to which you want to copy and press Enter to paste the content instantly.

MAIN DISH	SIDE DISH 1
Nachos Grande	▾
Aloha Chicken	Sticky White Rice
Grilled Italian Chicken	Pesto Couscous
Shish Kebabs	Sticky White Rice
Brown Sugar & Spice Rubbed Baby Back Ribs	Seasoned French Fries
Beef and Mushroom Skillet Supper	
Shrimp Fettuccini Pasta	Berries & Lemon Curd

Above: Excel adds a moving dotted line around cells that have been selected.

- **Paste**: Once the data is cut or copied, select the destination cell (or the first cell in a range) and press Ctrl + V.

○ **Cancel**: To stop a cut
or copy instruction,
press Escape.

Right-click Shortcuts

Select the cell(s), right-click
inside them and choose Cut
or Copy from the menu that
appears. Right-click in the
destination cell(s) and choose
Paste from the pop-up menu.

Toolbar Buttons

The Cut, Copy and Paste
toolbar buttons are on the
Home tab at the top left
of the Ribbon.

Hot Tip

Cells can be moved by
selecting them, then
pressing Shift and
Delete. Move to a
destination cell and
press Enter/Return to
paste the data.

PASTE SMART TAGS

When data is pasted into Excel, a Smart Tag appears in the bottom-right corner. Click it to access the drop-down menu with a variety of Paste options that can also help fix issues such as narrow column widths or incorrect formatting.

DELETING DATA

There are several ways of deleting cells. The method you choose should be guided by what it is that needs deleting.

Above: After pasting data into a cell, a Smart Tag appears with various Paste options.

Hot Tip

Do not use the space bar to delete cells. This overwrites the cell with a space and removes the contents, but it leaves unwanted spaces within the cell.

Deleting Cell Contents

The quickest way of deleting the contents of cells (without changing the formatting) is to select them and press the Delete key.

Deleting Cell Formatting

Select the relevant cells, click the Home tab, then in the Editing section, click Clear and select Clear Formats from the pop-up menu.

Deleting Rows and Columns

The simplest way is to right-click the row number or column letter and choose Delete from the menu that appears.

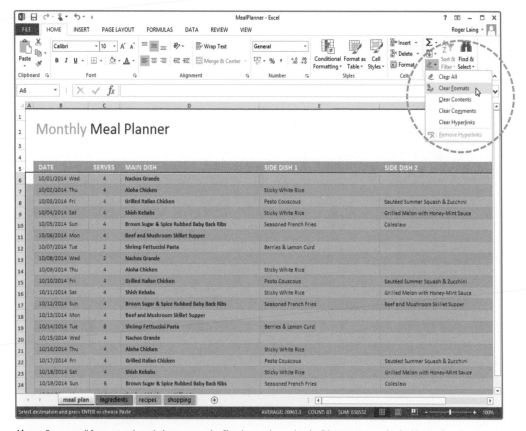

Above: Remove cell formatting through the menu on the Clear button, located in the Editing section under the Home tab.

EDITING DATA

If you need to edit or amend the contents of a cell, use one of the following shortcuts:

- **Press F2**: A flashing cursor appears inside the selected cell. Edit its contents using the arrow keys, Delete and Backspace.

- **Double-click**: Do this inside the cell that needs to be edited and a flashing cursor will appear where the mouse pointer was positioned.

- **Formula bar**: Select the cell to be edited. Its contents will be displayed in the Formula bar. Move the mouse pointer into the Formula bar and it will change to an I-beam. Left-click once to begin editing.

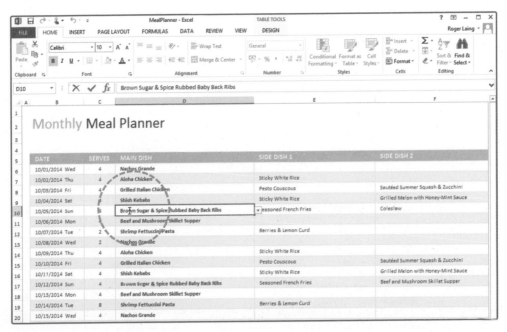

Above: When you want to change the content, double-click inside the cell and you can edit it there or in the Formula bar.

CHANGING ROWS AND COLUMNS

Columns and rows can be altered to fit their contents or the data available. Additional rows and columns can be inserted or removed to add more data or remove unwanted sections.

CHANGING COLUMN WIDTH

Select the column that needs to be widened or narrowed and move the mouse pointer to the right of the column letter. Once it changes to a black cross with double horizontal arrows, do one of the following:

- **Double-click**: The width of the column automatically resizes to fit the widest data.

- **Click and drag**: Move the cross pointer to the left to reduce the width of the column, or right to widen it.

CHANGING ROW HEIGHT

To alter a row's height, use the same techniques as for changing the width of a column.

Right: To adjust the column width, start by positioning the mouse pointer to the right of the column heading.

SELECTING MULTIPLE ROWS OR COLUMNS

Multiple rows can be resized at the same time and so can multiple columns. However, you cannot resize both multiple rows and columns together. To select a block of columns, left-click and swipe over the letters at the top. To select columns that aren't adjacent (such as columns A, G and Z), highlight the first column letter, hold down the Ctrl key and then select the remaining columns that you need.

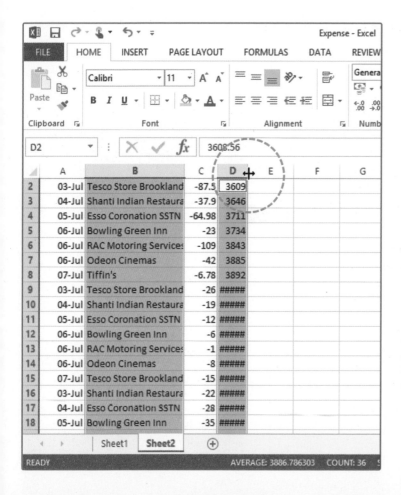

The same process can be used with rows. Once selected, resize one column or row using the technique shown above and the changes will be applied to the others.

Hot Tip

To select several rows or columns together, click one, then hold down the Shift key and use the arrow keys to select more.

Left: Selecting multiple columns (even if they are not adjacent) allows them to be resized at the same time.

INSERTING ROWS AND COLUMNS

There are two quick methods for adding extra rows and columns within a spreadsheet:

Right-click

Position the mouse pointer below the row number or to the right of the column letter where you want to add the extra row or column. Right-click and choose Insert from the pop-up menu.

Ctrl and +

Select the row or column where you want to add an extra one. Press Ctrl and the + key. An extra row or column will be inserted. If this does not work, press the Ctrl and Shift keys together, then the + key.

DELETING ROWS AND COLUMNS

Removing rows and columns is similar to inserting them. After right-clicking on a row number or column letter, choose Delete from the pop-up menu. Alternatively, select a row or column and press the Ctrl key and – (minus) key to remove it.

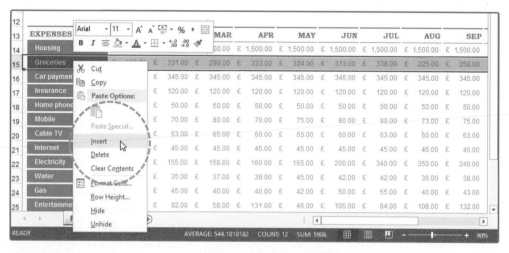

Above: Add an extra row by right-clicking on a row number and choosing Insert from the menu.

FORMATTING DATA

Excel contains a number of formatting tools to help you make sure important information is highlighted and easily visible.

FORMATTING TOOLBAR

This is accessed by clicking the Home tab. Select the cells you want to change, then use the command buttons to apply the formatting you want, such as changing the font and size, making text italic and altering cell, border and text colour.

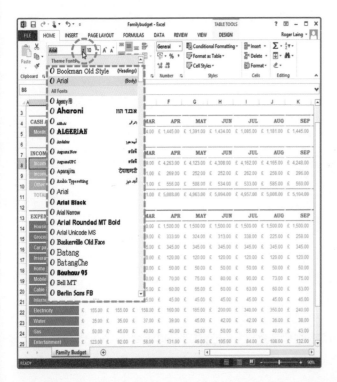

Fast Formatting

When editing a cell's contents, select the content you want to change and a small toolbar will appear with buttons to change the font, size, colour and other aspects. Alternatively, right-click inside a cell and the formatting toolbar will appear, along with a shortcut menu.

Left: The list of different fonts in Excel is displayed in alphabetical order, with a sample of each one.

> ## Hot Tip
> A quick way to make a cell's contents bold is to select the cell and press Ctrl + B. Repeat this to switch off bold.

FORMAT CELLS DIALOGUE BOX

The traditional method of changing the look of cells is to use the Format Cells dialogue box.

This can be opened by right-clicking inside a selected cell and choosing Format Cells. The dialogue box has a series of tabs to format numbers as currency, change alignment, add borders and more.

Setting Data to Currency

To set data to currency in the Format Cells dialogue box:

1. Click on the **Number tab**.

2. Find and select **Currency**.

3. Choose the number of **decimal places** (for example, 2 for amounts such as £1.50 and £150.00).

4. Select the **currency symbol**.

5. Choose a format for **negative values** (red and/ or with a minus symbol).

6. Click **OK**.

> ## Hot Tip
>
> **A quick way to open the Format Cells dialogue box is to press the Ctrl and Shift keys and the letter F.**

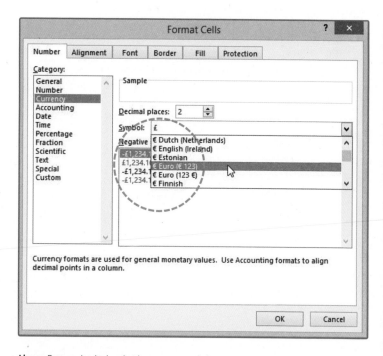

Above: Data can be displayed with a currency symbol by selecting it in the Format Cells dialogue box.

Setting a Percentage

When a percentage calculation is created, the result is not always automatically displayed as a percentage. You can press the % toolbar button or do the following:

- ⊙ Open the **Format Cells** dialogue box.

- ⊙ Click on the **Number** tab.

- ⊙ Select the **Percentage** option from the list on the left.

- ⊙ Choose the number of **decimal places** (for example, 2 for percentages to read 2.00%).

- ⊙ Click **OK**.

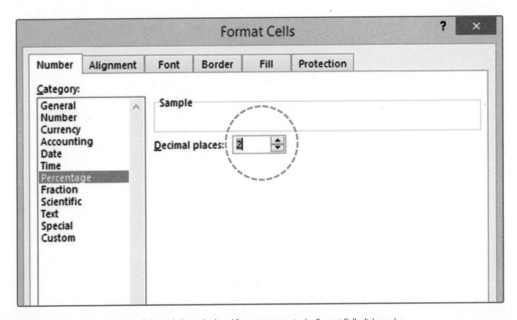

Above: You can alter the number of decimal places displayed for percentages in the Format Cells dialogue box.

Date Problems

If a date is entered into a cell, Excel will automatically format that cell to display it as a date. However, if a number is later entered into the cell, it may be converted into a date because Excel uses a number system for date calculations. To fix this problem:

- **Select** the cell in question.

- Open the **Format Cells** dialogue box.

- Click on the **Number** tab.

- Select **Number** from the list on the left.

- Choose the number of **decimal places**.

- Click **OK**.

Right: If a cell has previously been used for dates, it may have to be reformatted to enter a number instead.

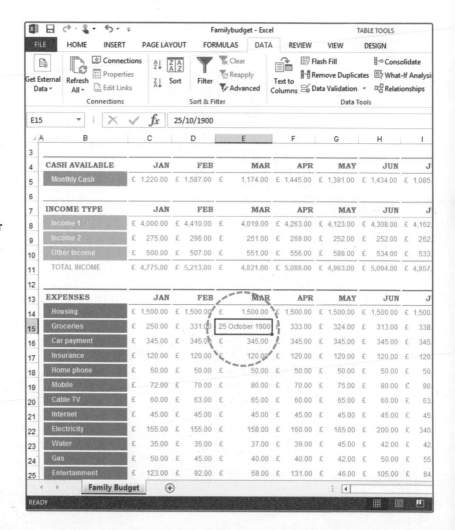

MAKING SENSE OF LARGE SPREADSHEETS

Navigating round a large spreadsheet can be difficult. However, Excel has a few techniques that save a lot of time and frustration.

ADJUSTING THE VIEW

Excel has some quick methods of zooming in and out of spreadsheets, and dividing up the view of one or several spreadsheets – all of which saves time on searching and scrolling through data.

Use the slider on the right-hand side of the Status bar to zoom in or out.

Splitting Up

If you need to view data that appears in two different parts of the same worksheet, you can split the sheet into two. To do so, select the row or column where you want the divide, click the View tab and press the Split button.

Freezing Panes

Listed data can often be difficult to understand and read if the headings aren't in view. Go to the View tab and click the Freeze Panes button. Select from the drop-down menu whether you want to keep the top column, first row or both onscreen while moving around a worksheet.

Hot Tip

Frozen panes can be spotted in a spreadsheet by a thicker line between the cells.

Hot Tip

To switch off Freeze Panes, simply select Unfreeze Panes from the drop-down menu.

Freeze Multiple Rows and Columns

Select a cell in the spreadsheet where the rows above it and the columns to the left need to remain onscreen, then select the Freeze Panes option as above.

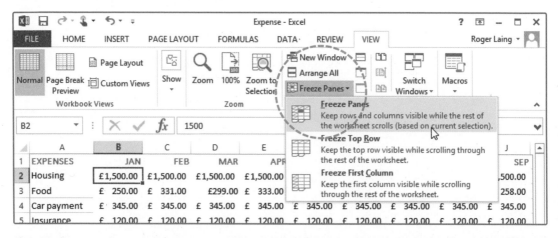

Above: The first row or column in a worksheet can remain visible onscreen when frozen, no matter how far down or across the screen you scroll.

VIEWING MORE THAN ONE SPREADSHEET

You can view more than one 'screen' at a time in Excel – whether it's different parts of the same worksheet or completely separate workbooks.

Make a New Window

If only one spreadsheet is open but you need to look at two different areas of it at once, click the View tab and press the New Window button. A second window showing the spreadsheet will open. Click the Arrange All button and, from the pop-up menu, choose how you want to organize the windows – for example, Vertical puts all the spreadsheets side by side onscreen – then click OK.

Working with More Than One Spreadsheet

Having several spreadsheets displayed onscreen makes it easier to check data and copy information. With the different spreadsheets open, click the Arrange All button, as above, to organize how they are displayed.

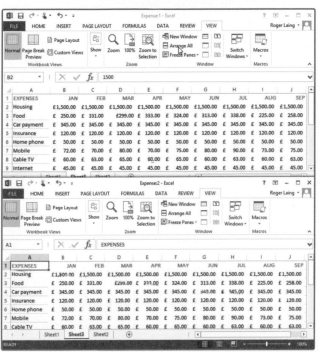

Left: Two or more views of the same worksheet can be set up in Excel by arranging windows.

HIDING ROWS AND COLUMNS

Rows and columns can be hidden so you see only essential data. Right-click on the column letter or row number and, from the menu that appears, choose Hide. To view it again, select the two columns or rows each side of it, right-click and choose Unhide.

Hot Tip

Several rows or columns can be hidden at the same time by selecting them, right-clicking and choosing Hide.

Below: Hidden rows or columns can be revealed by selecting the rows or columns either side, then right-clicking and choosing Unhide.

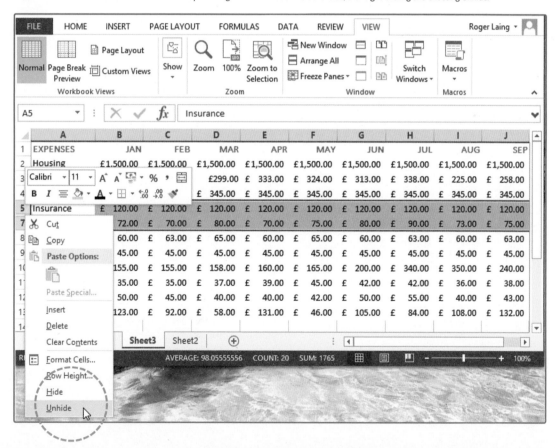

MANIPULATING LONG LISTS

Long lists of data often need to be trimmed or refined to extract the important data. This section shows the tools available in Excel.

FILTERING A LIST

Filters do not remove your data, but hide it or extract specific information based on a search. This is useful for ranking information, such as finding the best and worst results. On a downloaded bank statement, filtering can highlight particular transactions (direct debits for a pension, or wages payments, for example) or amounts under/over a specific value.

	Date	Store	Cost	Balance
1	Date	Store	Cost	Balanc
2	03-Jul	Tesco Store Brooklands	-87.5	3608.6
3	04-Jul	Shanti Indian Restaurant	-37.9	3646.5
4	05-Jul	Esso Coronation SSTN	-65	3711.4
5	06-Jul	Bowling Green Inn	-23	3734.4
6	06-Jul	RAC Motoring Services	-109	3843.4
7	06-Jul	Odeon Cinemas	-42	3885.4
8	07-Jul	Tiffin's	-6.78	3892.2
9	09-Jul	South-West trains	-26	3918.11
10	09-Jul	Pizza Express	-19	3937.21
11	12-Jul	Esso Coronation SSTN	-12	3949.54
12	13-Jul	Robert Dyas	-6	3955.07
13	14-Jul	RAC Motoring Services	-1	3956.07
14	14-Jul	iTunes	-8	3964.07

Above: AutoFilter is activated via the Filter button on the Data tab.

Instant AutoFilter

Excel's AutoFilter is one of its most useful features. It displays a
series of drop-down menus for each heading in a list, allowing
information to be filtered. To switch it on, make sure one cell
inside the list is selected, click the Data tab, then the Filter button.

Using AutoFilter to Find Information

When AutoFilter is activated, it adds a drop-down menu to each
heading. Click one of these and an alphabetically or numerically

Hot Tip

AutoFilter works
best if each
column in a list
has a heading.

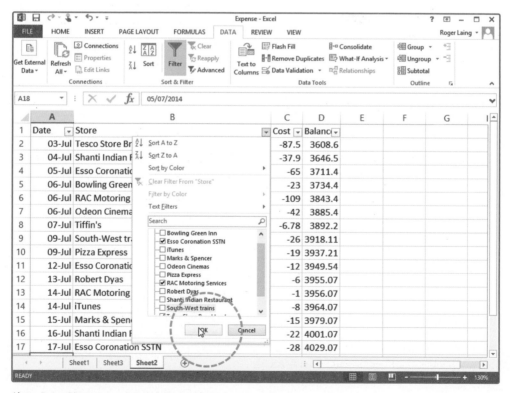

Above: In AutoFilter you can select which data to show.

sorted list of entries from that column will appear. Remove the tick marks to display only the rows of data in which this information exists.

Hot Tip

When using AutoFilter, if you want all the rows of data displayed – that is, no filtering – click on the Clear button.

Above: Values greater than a specific amount can be filtered, useful for seeing what all the big payments have been.

GREATER AND LESS THAN FILTERING

AutoFilter can be used to show specific dates, number ranges or amounts. This is useful when trying to find unpaid invoices issued before a specific date, for example, or high-value transactions on a bank statement.

Using Greater and Less Than Filtering

With AutoFilter on, click the drop-down menu to view a column listing dates or numerical values. Select Number Filters and a sub-menu appears. Choose one of the search options, such as Greater Than or Between.

A dialogue box will open, where you can enter specific values. Click on OK to see the results of the filter. To switch off this filter, return to the drop-down list and choose Select All from the tick-box list.

BEST AND WORST FIGURES

Filtering the best and worst results (also known as the Top 10) can show when a bank account was overdrawn, where sales figures are low and when expenditure is high. Select Number Filters followed by Top 10. In the dialogue box that appears, choose a Top or Bottom filter (best or worst results), followed by the number of items, then click OK.

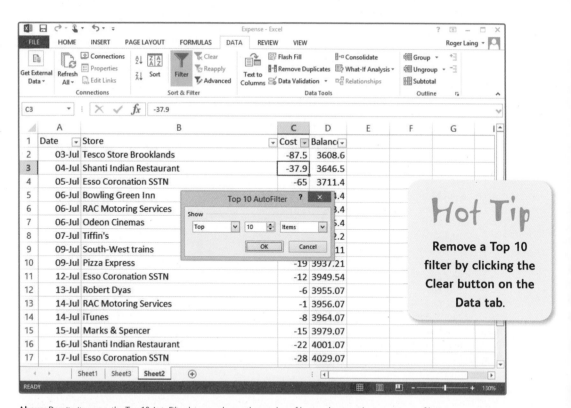

> **Hot Tip**
>
> Remove a Top 10 filter by clicking the Clear button on the Data tab.

Above: Despite its name, the Top 10 AutoFilter lets you choose the number of best and worst values you want to filter.

SORTING A LIST

Listed data can be sorted alphabetically or numerically to organize information in terms of the highest or lowest figures, for example, or the most recent.

BASIC SORTING

The following section explains how to sort your data and avoid some common pitfalls.

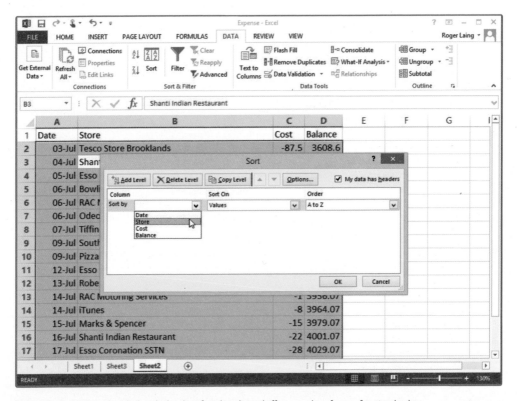

Above: The Sort dialogue box displays the headings found in a list and offers a number of ways of sorting the data.

Sorting

Select one cell inside the table or list of data that needs to be sorted. Click the Data tab, then the Sort button to open a Sort dialogue box. This offers three ways of sorting – by column heading, values or other criteria such as cell colour, and finally sort order. Make your selection and click OK.

Problems with Sorting

Excel will not always identify the cells contained inside a list, so column headings may be missed out or data will not be sorted. If this happens, try selecting all the data before opening the Sort dialogue box. If Excel does not recognize the column headings and consequently sorts them, double-check to ensure there is a tick against My data has headers in the Sort dialogue box.

FAST SORTING

The quickest way to sort is to select a cell inside the column to be sorted, then click either the Sort Ascending button (AZ icon with downward arrow) or Sort Descending button (ZA icon with downward arrow).

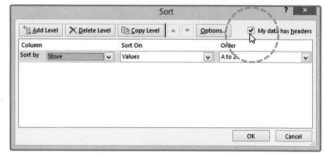

Above: To make sure that your headers are not sorted with the data, you need to tell Excel your data has headers.

Hot Tip

Undo is a life-saver when something goes wrong, because it reverses the mistake made. Activate it by pressing Ctrl + Z.

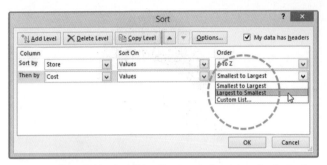

Above: Click on the Add Level button in the Sort dialogue box for Excel to sort on more than one column heading.

MULTIPLE SORTING

Excel can sort on more than one heading. For example, a list of sales results could be sorted in date order, but within each date, the sales values can be ordered numerically. Click the Add Level button in the Sort dialogue box and an extra row of sort criteria will be displayed.

SORT BY COLOUR

Lists of data can often be easier to understand if cells are colour-coded. For example, unpaid invoices could be coloured either red, orange or green to signify those that need attention.

Excel can then sort them according to their colours. When using the Sort dialogue box, change the Sort On (middle list) to Cell Colour, then specify which colour to use in the next drop-down list. Click on the Add Level button to enter further sort criteria for other colours.

Above: Sorting by colour is a good way to quickly find overdue or large payments.

Hot Tip

Click the Delete Level button in the Sort dialogue box to remove any sort criteria.

TALLYING DATA

Listed data can be grouped together and summarized to show totals and other calculations using Excel features such as Subtotals and PivotTables.

SUBTOTALS

Once you have a list, you can organize it in various ways to reveal different information, such as here with Subtotals.

Sort It First

Excel's Subtotals requires your data to be sorted, so that particular types of information are grouped together in one column. A list of expenses, for example, could be sorted so that all the entries that fall under different categories, such as mortgage, utility bills, food and petrol, are grouped with each other in the 'Type of Expense' column.

Choose the Numbers

Once a list of data has been sorted, make sure you have at least one column containing numbers that can be subtotalled. In a list of expenses, this might be the amount spent. In a list of sales, it could be columns for net amounts, VAT and gross amounts or all three.

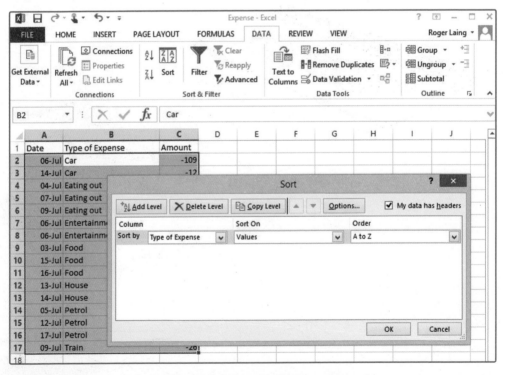

Above: A list needs to be sorted before it can be subtotalled, to ensure that data is correctly grouped.

Switch on Subtotals

Select one cell inside the list or, better still, all the data
to be included in the subtotal, plus the column headings.
Click the Data tab, the Outline button and then click the
Subtotal button to open a dialogue box.

Subtotal Dialogue Box

The Subtotal dialogue box has three main sections.
Starting at the top, choose the column heading that has been sorted and grouped. In the
section headed 'Use function', choose a calculation to apply (for example, Sum or Average).

> ## Hot Tip
>
> Select all the data by clicking one
> cell inside the list, then pressing
> Ctrl, Shift and the space bar.

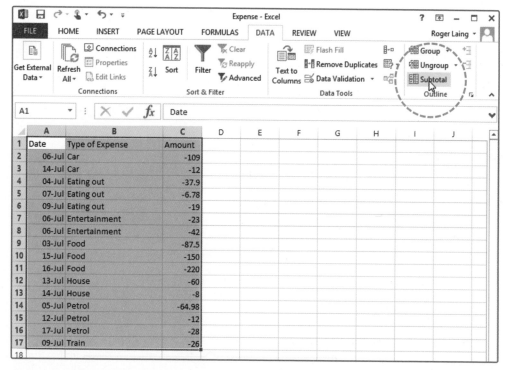

Above: Subtotal is activated by clicking the Subtotal button on the Data tab.

In the next section (Add subtotal to), make sure there is at least one tick mark against a column heading that contains numbers. Remove any tick marks against columns that don't have numbers (Excel sometimes adds them by accident). Click OK to see if the Subtotals have been correctly applied.

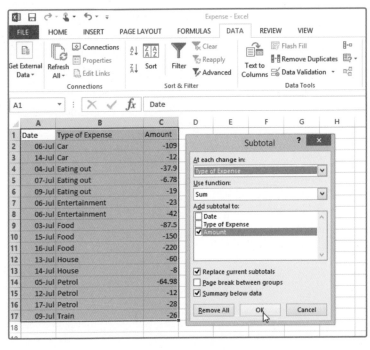

Above: The Subtotals feature can do various calculations on your data once it's sorted.

Using Subtotals

Once Subtotals have been applied, a series of numbered buttons appear at the top-left corner of the spreadsheet. Click button number 1 to show just the Grand Totals, or click button number 3 to display all the data. Alternatively, click the plus and minus symbols on the left of the screen to expand and collapse sections of data.

Non-Numerical Subtotals

Subtotals can be applied to lists that don't contain any numbers. Sort the information into relevant groups, open the Subtotal dialogue box and, under Use function, choose Count. This is useful for a to-do list, where Subtotals can show how many jobs there are for the house, garden, garage or car.

> ## Hot Tip
> The data in a list is not affected by applying or removing Subtotals.

Subtotals within Subtotals

A list can have more than one level of subtotals. For example, household expenses can have subtotals for the expenditure per month, as well as subtotals for how much has been spent on food, petrol and utility bills.

Removing Subtotals

This is easily done by selecting one cell inside the list, reopening the Subtotal dialogue box and clicking Remove All.

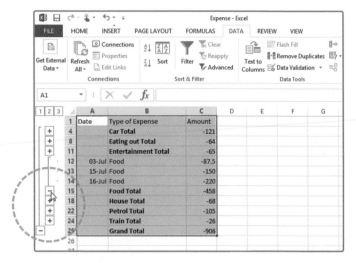

Above: After applying Subtotals to a list, click on the + and − symbols on the left side of the screen to expand and contract groups of data.

PIVOTTABLES

While Excel's Subtotals are useful for grouping and tallying data within a list, PivotTables are more powerful. They can summarize data in a separate area of a spreadsheet, without risk of anything happening to the original data.

Understanding PivotTables

PivotTables can summarize thousands of lines of information into one simple table. They should only be used for listed data, such as a downloaded bank statement, expenses list or sales data.

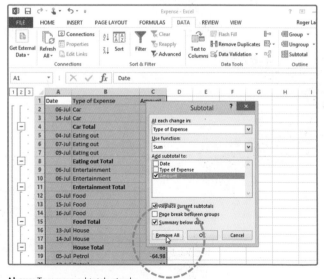

Above: To remove subtotals, simply open the Subtotal dialogue box and click Remove all.

Check Your Data

Your listed data should have headings across the top and the information underneath. There should be few or no blank cells and no blank rows.

Creating a PivotTable

Follow these steps to create a PivotTable:

1. It is a good idea to **select all the data** you're going to use before creating a PivotTable.

2. Click the **Insert** tab, then the **Tables** button.

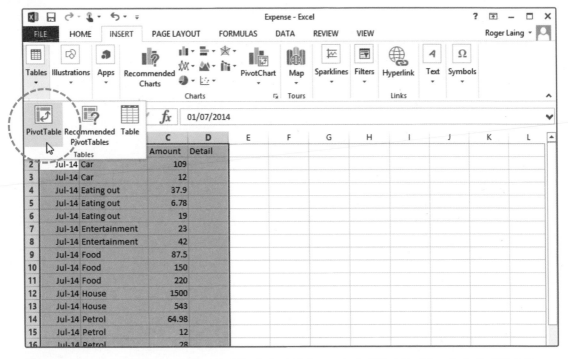

Above: Start creating a PivotTable by selecting the data, clicking the Insert tab, then pressing the Tables button followed by the PivotTable button.

▷↘ Press the **PivotTable** button to open the **Create PivotTable dialogue box**.

◁↘ **Check** the range of cells displayed is correct.

▽↘ Decide on the **location** for the PivotTable, which can be an existing worksheet or a new one that opens in the workbook being used.

▷↘ Click **OK**. A blank PivotTable opens with a number of options displayed on the right.

Hot Tip

Column headings containing amounts (numbers) are best placed in the Values part of a PivotTable.

Building a PivotTable

After creating an empty PivotTable, tick the column headings you want to use on the right-hand side of the screen (under PivotTable Fields). Data from the chosen columns is then added to the PivotTable, but it may not be displayed the way you want. At the bottom-right corner of the screen, you'll see the current layout. For example, the column headings are displayed under Values, with the summarized Values shown under Columns. Drag and drop the labels for these into a different section to change the layout of the PivotTable.

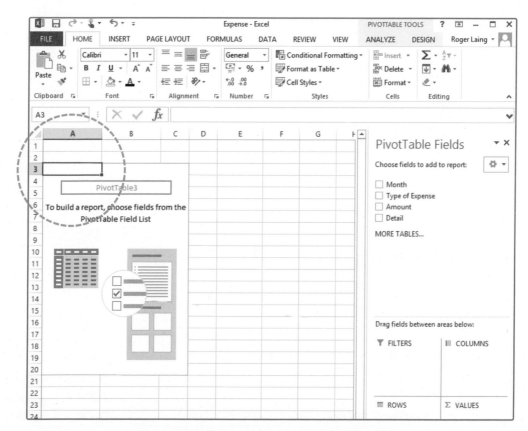

Above: Start building the PivotTable by selecting the columns you want to add from the PivotTable Fields.

Changing the PivotTable Calculation

The calculation usually used in a PivotTable is the Sum function for numbers (which totals them up) or Count for non-numerical data. To change this, right-click in a PivotTable cell that shows a calculation (a value). Choose Value Field Settings from the pop-up menu and, from the dialogue box that opens, select a different type of calculation for summarizing the data.

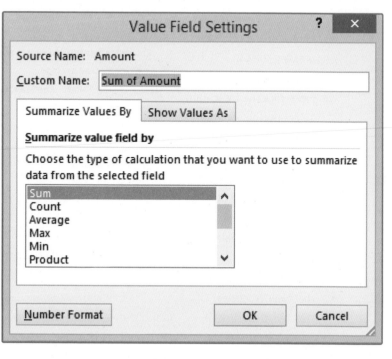

Above: In the Value Field Settings dialogue box you can change the type of calculation you want to use to summarize the data.

Step-by-Step: Making a PivotTable from Expenses

1. If you don't have a list to use, enter four headings in cells A1, B1, C1 and D1 with the words Month, Expense, Amount and Details. Type some sample data, making sure the dates in column A use the same format, such as Jan 14 or Mar 14.

Not sure whether a value inside a PivotTable is correct? Double-click on it and all the data that has been used to calculate that value will be displayed in a new worksheet.

2. Select the entire list by choosing one cell, then pressing the Ctrl + Shift keys and space bar. Next, click the Insert tab, Tables button and then the PivotTable button.

3. A Create PivotTable dialogue box will open. Make sure the cell references for Table/Range are correct (don't worry about the $ signs) and that New Worksheet is selected, then click OK.

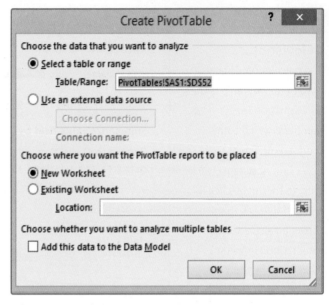

Create PivotTable   ?   ✕

Choose the data that you want to analyze

◉ Select a table or range

Table/Range: PivotTables!SAS1:SDS52

○ Use an external data source

Choose Connection...

Connection name:

Choose where you want the PivotTable report to be placed

◉ New Worksheet

○ Existing Worksheet

Location:

Choose whether you want to analyze multiple tables

☐ Add this data to the Data Model

OK   Cancel

Step 3: Make sure the cell reference is correct before you create the PivotTable.

4. A new blank PivotTable will open in a new worksheet. Check the box beside Month, Expense and Amount in the panel on the right.

Hot Tip

PivotTable data is not automatically updated, so right-click inside the PivotTable and choose Refresh.

5. The PivotTable is instantly constructed after clicking each field. However, the structure may not be right. If the Month heading is under Rows, drag and drop it to the Columns section.

6. Now click the AutoFilter triangles next to Row Labels and Column Labels (inside the PivotTable). A menu will drop down, allowing specific months or expense categories to be filtered.

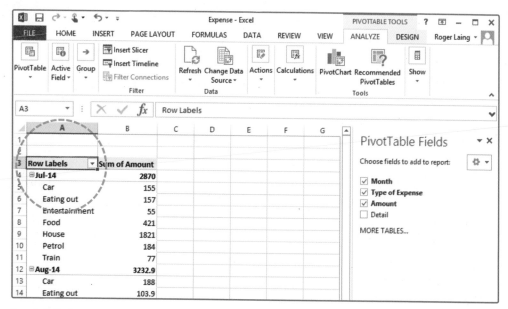

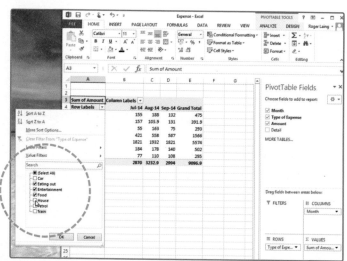

Step 5: Although the PivotTable appears instantly, you may want to change its layout.

7. To remove PivotTables, select the respective cells and press Delete on the keyboard, or right-click the PivotTable's sheet tab and choose Delete (all the data on that sheet will be lost).

Step 6: Filter the PivotTable to show only some of the key expense categories where spending can be cut back.

		1,250,000	45
Less sales returns and allowances		180,000	60
Net sales		1,070,000	1

Cost of Sales		Current Month	
		Amount	% of Sale
Beginning inventory		540,000	1
Plus goods purchased/manufactured		123,000	0
Total goods available		200,000	0
Less ending inventory		38,000	0
Total cost of goods sold		20,000	0
Gross profit (loss)		1,050,000	1

Operating Expenses		Current Month	
		Amount	% of Sales
Selling			
Salaries and wages		122,000	0
Commissions		112,000	
Advertising		335,000	
Depreciation		10,000	
Total selling expenses		579,000	
General/Administrative			
Salaries and wages		20,000	
Employee benefits		33,000	
Payroll taxes		70,000	
Insurance			
Rent			
Utilities			
Depreciation			
Office			

6 203	65 940	41 066
7 240	83 065	37 386
41 646	41 600	20 220
46 422	91 901	1 342
35 047	8 870	44 872
69 163	87 626	51 720
53 213	10 939	19 544
15 193	48 940	63 118
98 933	37 995	70 93
95 403	42 783	54 1
49 112	7 210	80 8
76 731	33 866	25
58 021	53 014	
83 612	23 076	
57 226	63 593	
39 344	42 234	
47 642	90 208	
44 279	85 507	
28 452	18 403	
43 797	6 484	
89 567	20 88	
34 828	84 8	
1 124	81	
93 124	35	
19 027	3	
62 934		
1 656	18 884	
81 562	47 368	
58 966	58 330	
20 609	95 924	
57 882		

ADVANCED EXCEL

MAKING YOUR OWN CALCULATIONS

Calculations can be written into a cell in Excel, but there are some important rules to be aware of and some potential problems that can arise.

BASIC RULES

There are a couple of fundamental rules that apply to Excel calculations.

Use the = Sign

Calculations in Excel must always begin with an equals (=) sign. This tells Excel that it is a calculation rather than text. For example, enter A1+B1 into a cell without the = sign and the text A1+B1 will be displayed rather than the result of the calculation.

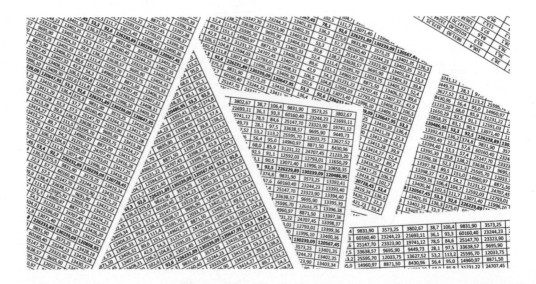

Select the Cells

When inputting a calculation, use the mouse to select the cells you want to include. This reduces the risk of errors.

MATHEMATICAL SYMBOLS

Excel uses the standard computer-based mathematical symbols for calculations. The + and - symbols are used for addition and subtraction, while the multiplication symbol is an asterisk (*). The division symbol is the forward slash (/).

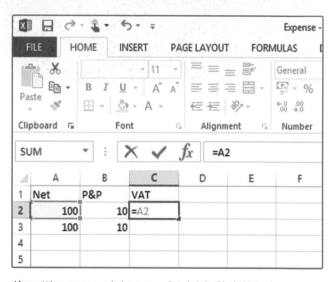

Above: When creating a calculation, any cells included will be highlighted with a coloured border.

BODMAS RULES

BODMAS is a mathematical rule covering the order in which calculations are carried out.

The abbreviation stands for:

Brackets
Of / **O**ther / **O**rder (exponents, such as powers and roots)
Division
Multiplication
Addition
Subtraction

Anything in brackets is calculated first. Inside the brackets, a division is calculated before a multiplication, then anything with an addition or subtraction. It is the same if there are no brackets – divisions and multiplications are calculated before additions and subtractions.

How BODMAS Works

The easiest way to understand this rule is to take the example of buying something on the Internet. The net price is listed, followed by a charge for postage and packing, then a calculation for VAT. Assume the net price is £100 and the postage is £10. If a calculation to work out the amount of VAT is written as =100+10*20%, then the BODMAS rule means multiplication comes first, so 10 will be multiplied by 20%. However, we need to add 100 and 10 together *before* multiplying by 20%, so the calculation needs to be written as =(100+10)*20%.

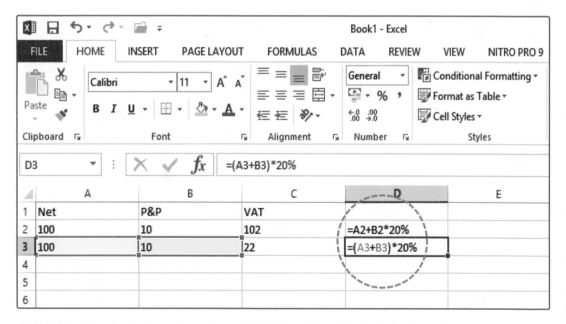

Above: The calculation result in C2 is wrong because the rule of BODMAS means 10 is multiplied by 20% first, whereas the calculation needs to add 100 and 10 first. Adding brackets resolves this.

DOLLAR SIGNS

Some calculations are created with dollar signs next to the cell references. These are known as 'absolute cell references' and mean that part or all of the cell reference will not change if it is copied elsewhere. It can be useful when multiple calculations are created using one cell, such as a single VAT value. If VAT changes, then there is only one cell to change.

When to Use Dollar Signs

If a list of product prices needs an adjacent column with a calculation for VAT, then a single cell can display the VAT amount. In the example pictured, cell E1 contains the VAT value.

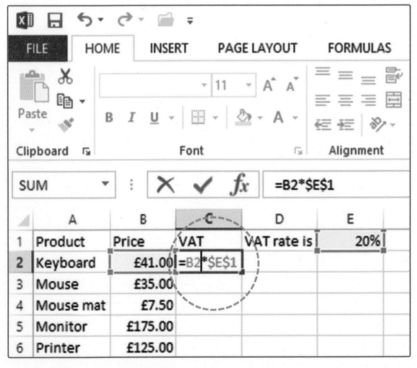

When the first VAT calculation is written in cell C2, it should read =B2*E1, but if this calculation is copied down the table, then the VAT calculation for the Mouse in C3 would read =B3*E2, which is wrong (E2 is empty). By changing the first calculation to read =B2*E1 the cell reference for E1 won't change, but the cell reference for B2 will change to B3, B4, and so on.

Above: Adding dollar signs to the cell reference for E1 means that when the calculation is copied down the table, the reference to E1 won't change, while the reference to B2 will (to B3, B4, etc).

ADDING, AVERAGING AND COUNTING

Straightforward calculations – including adding up lists of numbers, finding an average, or revealing the highest and lowest values – can be quickly created or displayed in Excel.

QUICK CALCULATIONS ON THE STATUS BAR

The Status bar can be used to show a number of calculations based on a selection of cells.

First, select a range of cells containing numbers. Next, look at the Status bar at the bottom of the screen. It shows the average and total (SUM) of the cells as well as a count.

AUTOSUM

Excel's AutoSum button, which has the Greek sigma symbol (Σ) displayed by it, is accessed by the Formulas tab.

Using AutoSum to Add Lists of Numbers

Select an empty cell at the bottom of a list of numbers or to the right of them. Click the AutoSum button and Excel automatically creates an = SUM calculation showing the cell range. Press Enter/Return to finish.

6	Home pho	£	50.00	£	50.00	£	50.00	£	50.00	£	50.00	£	50.00	£	50.00	£ 50.00 £
7	Mobile	£	72.00	£	70.00	£	80.00	£	70.00	£	75.00	£	80.00	£	90.00	£ 73.00 £
8	Cable TV	£	60.00	£	63.00	£	65.00	£	60.00	£	65.00	£	60.00	£	63.00	£ 60.00 £
9	Internet	£	45.00	£	45.00	£	45.00	£	45.00	£	45.00	£	45.00	£	45.00	£ 45.00 £
10	Electricity	£	155.00	£	155.00	£	158.00	£	160.00	£	165.00	£	200.00	£	340.00	£ 350.00 £ 2
11	Water	£	35.00	£	35.00	£	37.00	£	39.00	£	45.00	£	42.00	£	42.00	£ 36.00 £
12	Gas	£	50.00	£	45.00	£	40.00	£	40.00	£	42.00	£	50.00	£	55.00	£ 40.00 £
13	Entertainm	£	123.00	£	92.00	£	58.00	£	131.00	£	46.00	£	105.00	£	84.00	£ 108.00 £ 1

Sheet1   Filter   **Status**   Sorting   Subtotals   Chec ...   ⊕

READY   AVERAGE: £241.08   COUNT: 12   SUM: £2,893.00

Above: Select a range of cells and a summary will be displayed on the Status bar, including a count of how many calculations there are, the average and the total.

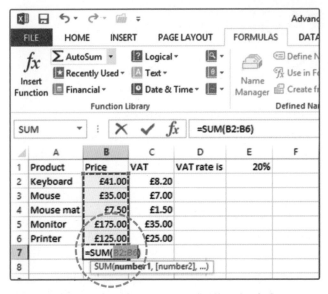

Above: Excel's AutoSum can automatically add up a list of cells.

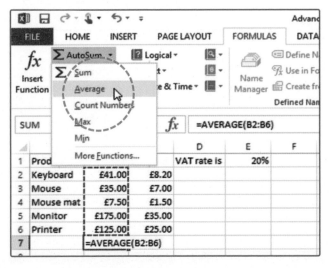

Above: Click on the arrow beside the AutoSum button for a drop-down menu of other types of calculation, such as Average.

Hot Tip

If the cell references are incorrect, all you need to do is select the correct ones to overwrite the calculation.

AutoSum an Entire Table

To add totals at the bottom and/or right of a table of numbers, select the table and an empty row of cells below it and/or to the right of it. Click the AutoSum button and the totals will be added to the empty cells selected.

Other Calculations with AutoSum

The drop-down menu on the AutoSum button has some additional calculations, including:

○ **Average:** The mean average value of the selected cells.
○ **Count Numbers:** The number of cells containing numbers.
○ **Max:** The highest number in a range of cells.
○ **Min:** the lowest number in a range of cells.

BASIC FUNCTIONS

Excel has a number of ready-to-use calculations called functions. These save time and have a wide range of uses, including statistical analysis, finding data in a list and error checking.

ADDING A FUNCTION TO A CELL

A function is entered and displayed inside a cell just like any other calculation. To add one, select the cell where you want the function displayed, then click the fx button in the Formula bar.

Choosing a Function

Clicking the fx button opens the Insert Function dialogue box. Use the Search box to type in what you want to do and Excel will make a suggestion.

Alternatively, you can select from a drop-down list that includes Most Recently Used or select the individual function you want. When you select a function, a definition will appear below it.

Filling in Function Boxes

After choosing a particular function from the list, click OK and the dialogue box will display a

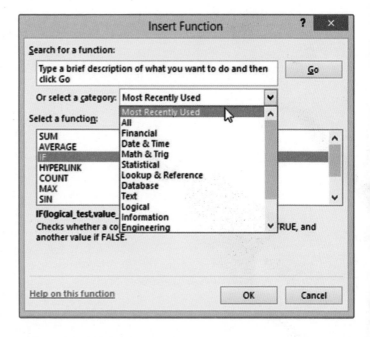

Above: The Function dialogue box separates all the functions into different categories to make them easier to find.

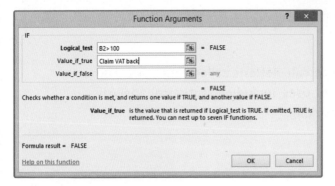

Above: Excel guides you through the process of entering function criteria, and displays results or error messages where appropriate.

box in which to enter the details needed. Add the cell ranges or select them for the information to be entered automatically. Excel guides you through setting up the function, displaying instant error messages if anything is wrong. Once correct, the result of the function is displayed inside the dialogue box.

Hot Tip

There's no need to start a function with an = symbol. Just click on the fx button.

Types of Function

There are thousands available in Excel, which are grouped into similar types of function for ease of reference.

- **Database functions**: Known as the DFunctions, these analyse data that's part of a list or database.

- **Date and time functions**: Can extract date and time values from cells in a worksheet, then use them for calculations.

- **Financial functions**: Perform popular business calculations, often related to borrowing or saving money.

- **Information functions**: Referred to as IS functions, these check the type of values in a selected cell and return TRUE or FALSE, depending on the outcome.

- **Logical functions**: These are used to test whether the contents of a cell meet specific conditions.

- **Lookup and reference functions**: Can locate a specific value from a list or find a reference for a specific cell.

> **Hot Tip**
>
> An old function can be edited by selecting its cell and clicking on the fx button.

- **Maths functions**: Perform both simple and complex mathematical calculations.

- **Statistical functions**: Range from the commonly used SUM and AVERAGE functions to the specialist, like the cumulative beta probability density function.

- **Text functions**: Allow cells to be combined, trimmed and calculated to help eliminate unwanted data.

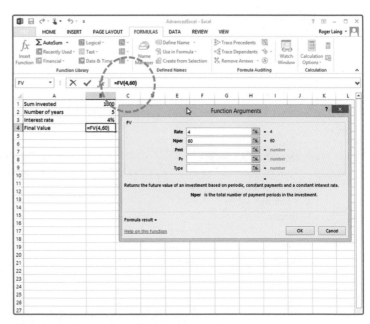

Above: The FV function, a financial function, can be used to calculate the final figure for a regular investment.

VLOOKUP FUNCTION

The Vlookup function is one of the most popular but confusing ones in Excel. It is useful for finding unique information in a long list, such as a product code or specific date.

UNDERSTANDING VLOOKUPS

Vlookup stands for Vertical Lookup. This function is a search method that can retrieve and display information from a list, along with related data from adjacent columns.

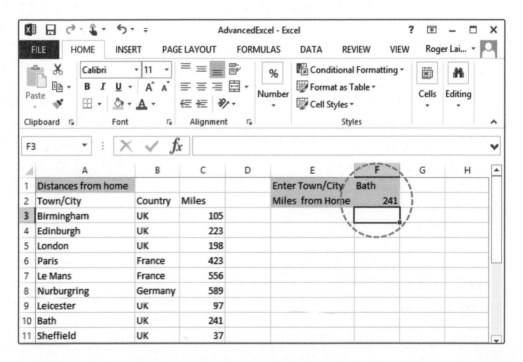

Above: In this Vlookup example, a town/city can be entered in cell F1 and the Vlookup in cell F2 will find the mileage from the list on the left.

Vlookup Rules

The following checklist will ensure your Vlookup function works correctly.

- ⊙ **List down:** A Vlookup searches *down* a list, so make sure your data is displayed as a list.

Hot Tip

If a list runs across the screen, not down, use the Hlookup (Horizontal Lookup) function.

- **Avoid blanks**: Make sure there are no blank rows.

- **First column**: This is the one searched, so make sure it contains the relevant data.

- **Unique or nearest match**: Vlookup searches for a unique entry, otherwise it will display the first or nearest match.

Step-by-Step: Creating a Vlookup

This guide shows how to create a list of favourite destinations and the corresponding distances to home. Rather than scroll up and down the list to search for a particular place, the destination can be entered in one cell and a Vlookup used to find that place in the list and display the mileage.

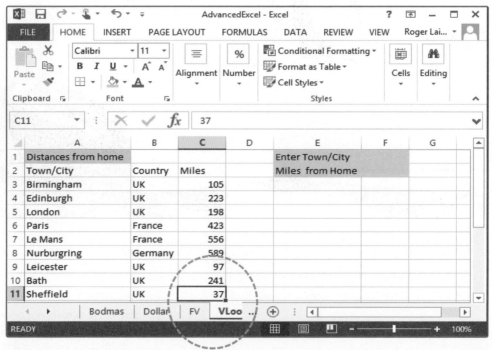

Step 1: In this example, the search data will be displayed in cell F1 and the Vlookup will be created in cell F2.

1. Enter a list of town and city names in column A, a corresponding list of countries in column B and the approximate distance from home to these places in column C. This table/list will be used by a Vlookup to find a particular town or city.

2. Enter the headings shown in the illustration for cells E1 and E2, then enter a town or city name from the table or list in cell F1. The data in cell F1 will be used by Vlookup to locate the relevant information in the list/table.

3. Select cell F2, where the Vlookup will be located. Click the fx button on the Formula bar or Toolbar. Vlookup may be listed in the dialogue box that appears. If not, change the Category to Lookup & Reference and scroll down the Select a function list. Select Vlookup and click OK.

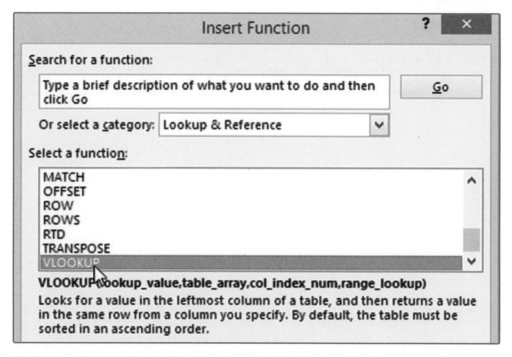

Step 3: Vlookup is listed under the Lookup & Reference category within the Insert Function dialogue box.

4. Click inside the first white box, labelled Lookup value, and select cell F1. Click inside the second white box (Table array) and select the cells containing the names of the cities/ towns, countries and miles. Click inside the third white box (Col index num) and type the number 3 (for the third column in the table). Finally, click in the last white box and type the word False (this will ensure an exact match is – see the picture below).

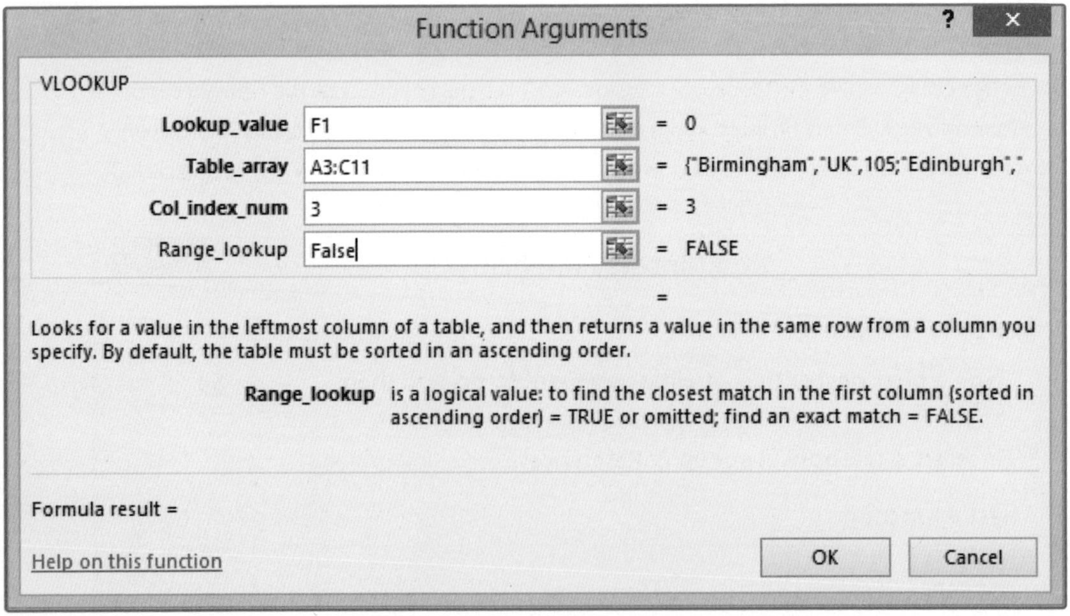

Function Arguments		? ✕
VLOOKUP		
Lookup_value	F1	= 0
Table_array	A3:C11	= {"Birmingham","UK",105;"Edinburgh","
Col_index_num	3	= 3
Range_lookup	False	= FALSE

=

Looks for a value in the leftmost column of a table, and then returns a value in the same row from a column you specify. By default, the table must be sorted in an ascending order.

Range_lookup is a logical value: to find the closest match in the first column (sorted in ascending order) = TRUE or omitted; find an exact match = FALSE.

Formula result =

Help on this function   OK   Cancel

Step 4: Entering the word 'False' in the Range_lookup section of a Vlookup ensures only an exact match is found.

5. After entering data in all four boxes, a result will be displayed in the dialogue box. If it's wrong, check the details entered and make sure the town/city entered in F1 is spelt correctly.

6. Click OK to close the dialogue box. Test the Vlookup by changing the town/city name in cell F1.

PRESENTING EXCEL DATA

You may want to use data from a spreadsheet in a presentation. Excel can help you present the information professionally.

CREATING CHARTS

Presenting data in a chart makes it easier to understand and spot trends. Here are some shortcuts to make an effective chart.

Hot Tip

Your data should ideally be displayed in a table with headings or row labels (or both). This makes it easier for Excel to produce a chart.

Press F11 or Alt + F1

One quick method for creating a chart is to select the data to include (plus any headings or row labels) and press F11.

The new chart will be displayed in a separate worksheet. If you want the chart to appear beside the selected cells, press Alt and F1 instead.

Changing the Chart Type

This is done by right-clicking on the Chart and choosing Change Chart Type. There are several different types of chart to

choose from – ranging from Pie charts to Line charts – in the dialogue box that opens. Within each chart category, there is also a choice of styles – such as 3D.

Add More Data

Right-click on the chart and choose Select Data, then change the Chart data range to cover all the cells required.

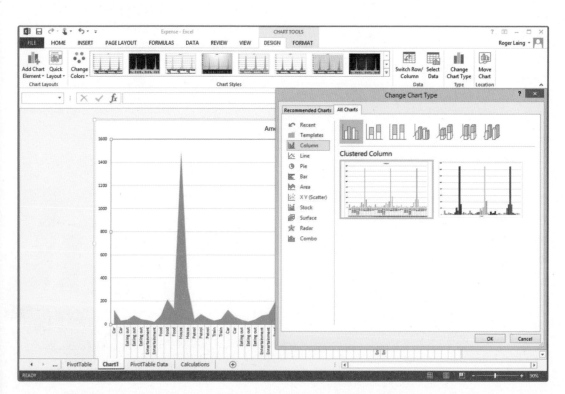

Above: Right-click on the chart and choose Change Chart Type to select the chart that best illustrates your data.

PRINTING EXCEL DATA

Excel spreadsheets can be printed out, but printing can be more problematic than with other types of file.

PRINTING TRICKS

There are several techniques to help ensure your printout is correctly laid out.

Check with Print Preview

Click the File tab and choose Print, which shows onscreen how the printout will look. You can also change various print settings.

- **Landscape to portrait**: Use the drop-down Orientation button.

- **Squeeze it in**: Click the Fit All Columns on One Page button and there are various options for shrinking the printout.

> ## Hot Tip
> The Quick Access Toolbar (top left of the screen) can display a Print Preview and Print button. Click on the drop-down arrow to display this button.

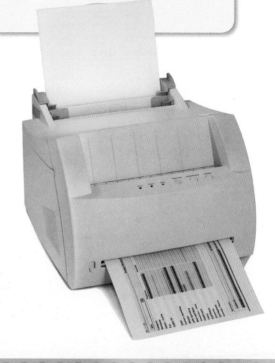

> ## Hot Tip
> Press Ctrl + F2 or Ctrl + P to open the Print and Print Preview screen.

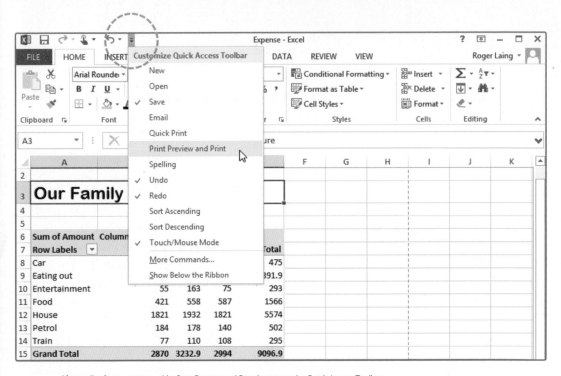

Above: For faster printing, add a Print Preview and Print button to the Quick Access Toolbar.

- ○ **Tweak the margins:** Click the Margins button and select your preferred option to increase or decrease the space at the bottom, top, left and right side of the page.

PRINTING ENHANCEMENTS

There are several features in Excel that can enhance the look of a printed spreadsheet.

Repeat Rows and Columns

A long list can be difficult to read if the headings or row labels are only displayed on the first page. To include them throughout your printout:

1. Click on the **Page Layout** tab and select the **Print Titles** button. The **Page Setup** dialogue box will open at the 'Sheet' tab.

2. Click the '**Rows to repeat at top**' box and select one cell in the row you want. The whole row will be printed.

3. Do the same for columns by clicking the '**Columns to repeat at left**' box.

4. Click **Print** and check in the print preview to see the headings and/or labels have been added to each page.

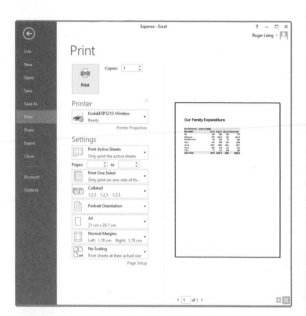

Above: The Print screen gives a Print Preview, showing how each page will be printed before it's sent to the printer.

Headers and Footers

Information can be printed at the top (header) and bottom (footer) of each page. This is useful if you want to add page numbers, your name and the date.

1. Click the **File** tab and select **Print**.

2. Press **Page Setup** to open the dialogue box.

3. Select the **Header/Footer** tab.

4. Choose different types of preset headers and footers from the **drop-down lists**.

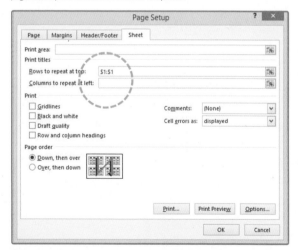

Above: Rows and columns can be repeated on every printed page, which helps with long lists or wide tables with headings or labels.

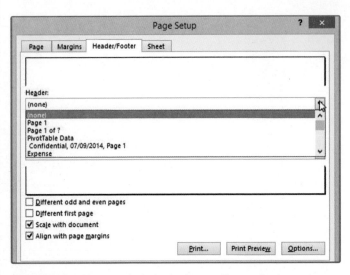

Above: Headers and footers can be displayed at the top and bottom of each printed page.

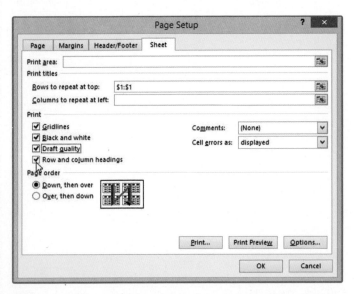

Above: The cause of poor-quality printing with no colour and missing gridlines can sometimes be found on the Sheet tab in the Page Setup dialogue box.

5. Alternatively, click the **Custom** buttons to write your own.

6. If headers and footers need to be **different on the first page** or on **odd and even pages** (useful when making a book), there are tick boxes for these options.

7. Click **OK** to finish.

PRINTING PROBLEMS

If things do go wrong with printing, this section will help you troubleshoot and find the solutions.

Blank Pages Printed

If one or more blank pages are printed, it means the print area for the worksheet is too large. The easiest way to fix this is to set the print area. Select the cells to be printed, click the Page Layout tab, choose the Print Area button and select Set Print Area from the drop-down menu.

Leftover Column Printed on a Separate Page

If a column on the far right of a table is printed on a separate page, change the scaling and margins to make sure it is included with the others.

Print Layout Errors

Several printout problems can be resolved by opening the Page Setup dialogue box (see page 101) and clicking the Sheet tab.

- ○ **Row and column headings are printed**: Remove the tick mark from beside Row and column headings.

- ○ **No gridlines**: Tick the box beside Gridlines to add them or uncheck to remove them.

- ○ **Poor-quality print**: Make sure there's no tick mark beside Draft quality.

- ○ **No colour**: Uncheck the box beside Black and white.

TROUBLESHOOTING

WARNING AND ERROR MESSAGES

Mistakes are easily made, but Excel has a range of messages to help pinpoint the problem and offer solutions.

CELL RESULTS ERRORS

Below are some common error messages, along with guidance on how to fix the issues.

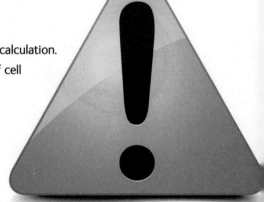

#NAME?

This means that Excel can't find a cell reference in a calculation. Check that all cell references are correctly entered. If cell names are used, check they are spelt consistently.

#VALUE!

If an amount displayed in a cell is not a number, date or time, then it cannot be used in a calculation or function. Consequently, a #VALUE? error will appear.

Typically, this is because there's text in the cell – possibly because of typing errors (100 has been entered as 1oo, for example) or imported data has been misinterpreted.

#N/A

This error message appears in cells containing a Vlookup function. If the data (lookup value) requested cannot be found, the 'not available' (#N/A) message is displayed instead. Usually the lookup value has been incorrectly entered.

#REF

The error message #REF shows that a column, row, worksheet or workbook referred to in a calculation has been deleted.

#DIV/0

The #DIV/0 error message will appear when a cell has been divided by zero or an empty cell. This type of problem often arises with imported data in which empty cells and rows exist.

#NULL!

The #NULL! error is displayed in functions such as SUM, where a cell range has been incorrectly entered. Reselect the correct range of cells to resolve this problem.

#NUM!

This shows a calculation or function contains invalid numeric values. To fix this, go back and check the values.

#####

This indicates that a cell is not wide enough to display all the characters for a number or date. This can easily be resolved by widening the column.

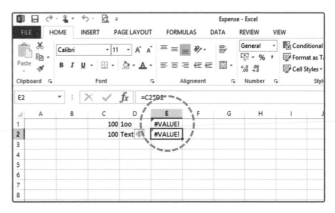

Above: Multiply 100 by a cell containing the word Text or a mistyped entry such as 1oo (instead of 100), and a #VALUE! error will be displayed.

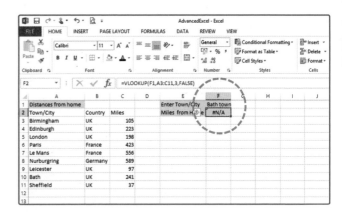

Above: The #N/A error message is displayed in this Vlookup because the wrong name for a town has been entered in the lookup value in cell F1.

Hot Tip

The ##### error message does not appear if text is too wide for a cell, only when it contains numbers.

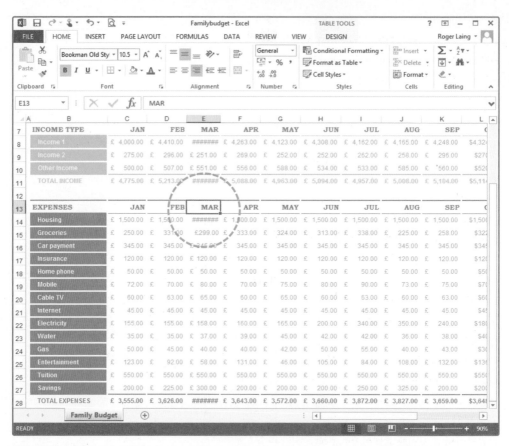

Above: If a cell containing a number or date is not wide enough, the value will be displayed as a series of # symbols.

CELL WARNING MESSAGES

As well as cell error messages, Excel has other warnings to alert you to potential problems.

Knock-on Errors

One error can result in another. If one cell refers to a cell that has an error, then this second cell will also display the same warning message.

Circular References

This is when a calculation includes a reference to the cell it is in. As well as the warning, arrows onscreen point to the problem cells.

Error Indicators

The error indicator is a green triangle in the top-left corner of a cell. Select the cell and an exclamation mark inside a yellow diamond will appear next to it.

Hover over this and a short message will appear explaining the problem. Click the exclamation mark and a variety of error-check options wil appear on the drop-down menu, including a link to help on the specific error.

WRONG WARNINGS

Excel sometimes wrongly identifies errors. As an example, take a list of values with a date at the top. If the list is totalled using the Sum function, Excel displays a warning message advising that the date isn't included in the calculation (it treats the date as a number). Click the exclamation mark and Excel will suggest that the date is included in the calculation. Choose this option and the calculation will be wrong. From the same drop-down menu, you can tell Excel to Ignore Error.

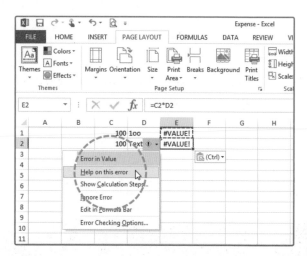

Above: Click the Exclamation Smart tag beside an error message and then on Help on this error to get more information on what's wrong.

Above: The list of numbers shown here has a date at the top with a Sum total at the bottom; Excel sees the date as a number and suggests it should be included in the Sum total.

EXCEL TROUBLESHOOTER

Like any computer program, Excel is not perfect. Here are some of the typical troubles you might experience.

CELL, COLUMN AND ROW ERRORS

When a cell's content is not displayed as it should be, there is usually a fairly simple solution.

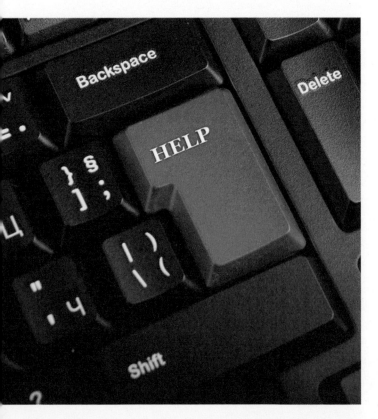

Date Turns into a Number

Excel stores dates as sequential serial numbers, so they can be used in calculations to work out differences. 1 January 1900, for instance, is serial number 1. 1 January 2008 is serial number 39,448 because it is that number of days after 1 January 1900. Sometimes, if a cell has been formatted as a number, any date entered is converted to its serial number equivalent.

To fix this, right-click the cell and choose Format Cells. In the dialogue box that opens, select the Number tab, then the Date option on the left and choose a date format.

Number Turns into a Date

In this case, a cell has been formatted as a date. When a number is entered, it is converted into a date. For example, 50,000 will become 21 November 2036. This can be fixed by right-clicking the cell, choosing Format Cells, then the Number option on the Number tab, and changing the format.

Hot Tip

To quickly format a cell for a date, number or other type, click the Home tab and select from the drop-down list in the Number section.

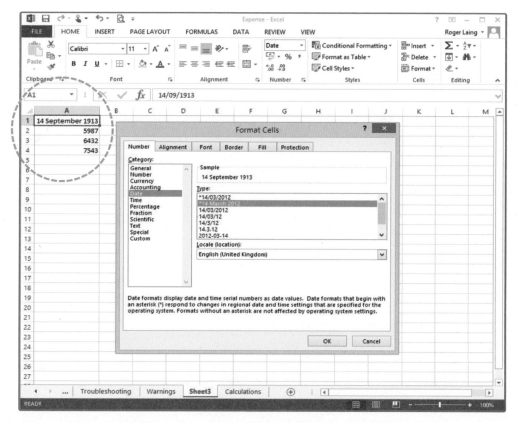

Above: Cells containing date formatting will convert a number into a date. Here, cell A1 has been formatted as a date, so when the number 5006 is inputted, the number is converted to a date.

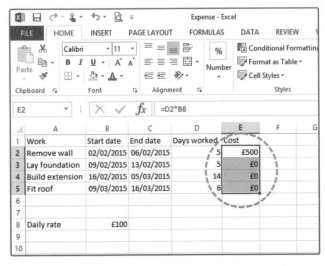

Above: The calculation copied from cell E2 will not work unless the reference to B8 is fixed with $ signs.

Copied Calculations Don't Work

If a copied calculation needs to refer to the same cell in each calculation, the absolute cell reference should be fixed with dollar signs (for example, B8). The illustration shows a calculation for cost of work in column E, based on a fixed daily rate of £100 (in B8), and a list of days worked in column D. The first calculation in E2 reads =D2*B8, but when copied, the next calculation reads =E3*B9, which is wrong (there's nothing in B9). Writing

the first calculation as =E2*B8 will fix this problem. Copy the calculation and the reference to B8 will not change.

Copied Data is Incorrectly Formatted

This often occurs when copying data from another program or from a website. The pasted data may be too narrow for the columns, or may be in the wrong font and size. Click the Smart Tag at the bottom-right corner of the pasted cells. A menu will open with options for changing the cell formatting.

> ### Hot Tip
> When writing a calculation that needs to include $ signs, type the cell reference and press F4 to add them. Note that this only works with calculations.

COMMON PROBLEMS AND SIMPLE SOLUTIONS

When there's a problem, Excel can be very frustrating, but there's usually a quick and easy way to resolve it and complete your task.

Missing Ribbon

Excel groups sets of buttons on the Ribbon under different tabs (File, Home, Formulas and so on). If only the tabs are visible, it's likely that the

> ### Hot Tip
> Excel displays a small arrow in the top-right corner of the screen, which can be used to collapse the Ribbon.

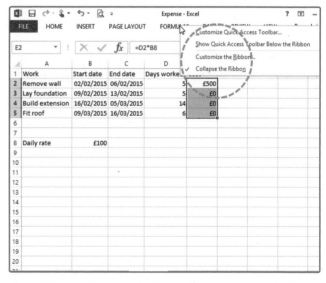

Above: If the Ribbon disappears, right-click any tab and deselect Collapse the Ribbon.

Ribbon has been minimized. Right-click any tab and remove the tick mark beside Collapse the Ribbon by selecting this option.

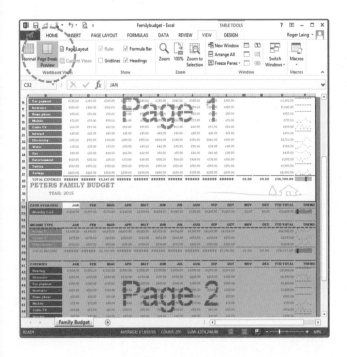

Above: In Page Break Preview the spreadsheet can look confusing, so select Normal to go back to the standard view.

Hot Tip

Hold down Alt + the Tab key to switch between programs and files.

Missing Cells and Page 1 Displayed across the Worksheet

This suggests that Page Break Preview, which shows the number of pages that will be printed and what will be included on each one, has been selected in error. This view also hides rows and columns that will not be printed. To return to the standard view, click the View Ribbon tab and select the Normal button.

Where Are Recently Opened Files?

If not all of your files are visible onscreen, click the View tab and select the Switch Windows button. A list of open Excel files will be displayed. Simply select one to view it.

Cells Cannot Be Changed

This usually means that the worksheet has been 'protected' to prevent the data from being changed (although it may still be possible to edit some cells). To remove protection, right-click the open sheet tab and see if the words

Unprotect Sheet are displayed on the shortcut menu. If they are, select this option. Provided the sheet has not been protected with a password, it should be unlocked.

Renaming a Sheet Tab

Right-click on the sheet tab and choose Rename. Type the new name and press Enter/Return. Alternatively, double-click the sheet tab and overwrite the name there.

Hot Tip

Insert an extra worksheet by pressing Shift + F11.

Add More Sheets to a Workbook

Click on the small Insert Worksheet button to the right of the sheet tabs.

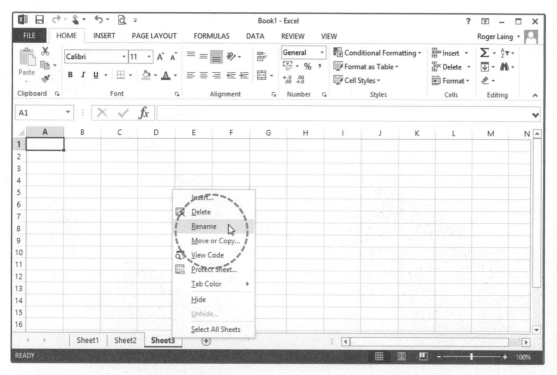

Above: Sheet tabs can be renamed by right-clicking and selecting Rename from the shortcut menu.

EXCEL ON THE GO

MOBILE EXCEL

Even if you're away from your PC, you can still access your Excel files using special versions of the program available for tablets and smartphones, or through Excel Online.

USING EXCEL ON YOUR TABLET

Lightweight they may be, but tablets can still do most of the heavyweight work needed to create and edit Excel on the go. The different Excel apps available have many of the features of the desktop version.

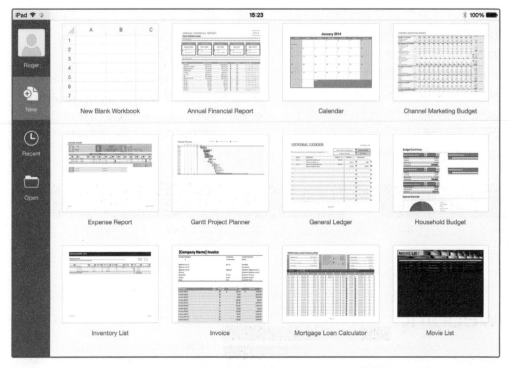

Above: When you open a new file, you will see that the iPad version of Excel has most of the same templates as available on the desktop.

Windows Tablets

These run the same version of Excel 2013 as you have on your desktop computer, although it has been made more touch friendly.

The buttons on the Ribbon are slightly larger and more spaced out to make it easier for fingertip control.

iPad

There's now a specific Excel app for the iPad. While it's free if you only want to look at your Excel files, you'll have to subscribe to Office 365 to create or edit documents.

When you open Excel on the iPad, you'll notice the Ribbon is more like a traditional toolbar. Tap an icon and a drop-down menu will open with the various options. Although the Excel app doesn't have all the features available in the desktop version, it has enough to carry out most everyday tasks.

Hot Tip

Although there's no Microsoft version of Excel for Android tablets, there are plenty of third-party apps available that can work with the Office spreadsheets.

Above: The Ribbon on the iPad version of Excel is more like a traditional toolbar, with buttons to tap to access core features.

EXCEL FOR SMARTPHONES

There is not a separate smartphone version of Excel – it is included in the Office Mobile app. Although free for home use, you need an Office 365 subscription for business use.

Using the App

- You can **view**, **create** and **edit** your workbooks.

- View your files on your smartphone **just as they are on your desktop**, including any charts.

> ### Hot Tip
>
> There are Office Mobile apps, including Excel, for all Windows Phones, the iPhone and later Android phone models.

- You can add basic functions, like **AutoSum**, **sort lists** and **format cells**. For example, on an Android phone, with a spreadsheet open, tap the More menu (three vertical dots) and select Format cell. Here, you can change cell content to a date, currency, percentage or number, as well as format text and alter colours.

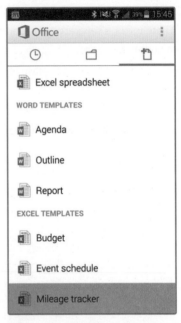

EXCEL BY TOUCH

Some of the latest features in Excel are designed for touch screens.

Above: As part of the Office app for smartphones (here, it's the Android version), Excel will let you view, create and edit worksheets.

Touch Gestures

Typical touch-screen gestures – including tap, pinch, stretch, slide and swipe for zooming into spreadsheets or moving between worksheets – are available in Excel. Go to the Quick Access Toolbar and click the arrow beside the hand icon and select Touch. This spreads out the command icons on the Ribbon so they're easier to use with touch.

Select a Range

Tap a cell, then drag a selection handle over the cells you want.

AutoFill

Tap the cell(s) with the content you want to copy. Tap again and, in the menu that opens, tap AutoFill. Drag the downward-pointing arrow to fill the cells.

Above: Basic formatting tools allow you to change the size of text, add colour, and more.

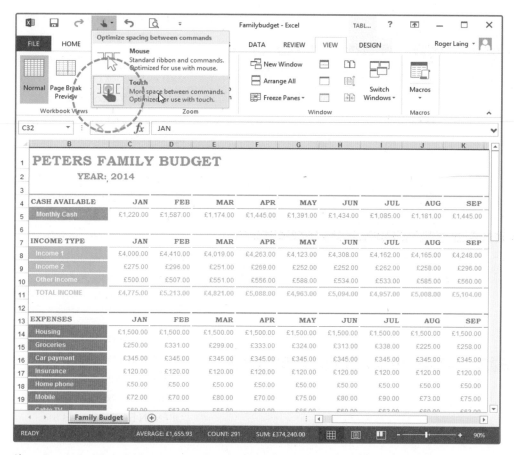

Above: From the Quick Access Toolbar you can spread out the command buttons to make them easier to use with touch.

Edit a Cell

Double-tap a cell to be able to edit its contents.

Step-by-Step: Microsoft Excel Online

Excel is part of Office Online, which allows you to work on your documents through a browser on any PC or mobile device. Start by going to Office.com.

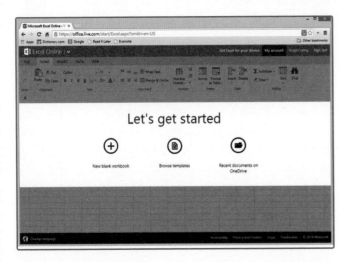

Above: To start, you can set up a new workbook, choose a template or open an existing file from OneDrive.

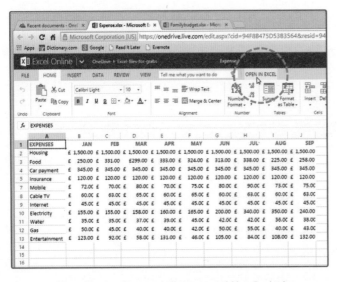

Above: If you need commands that are not available in Excel online, you can open it in the desktop version of Excel.

1. You will need to sign in with your Microsoft account. You will have one if you use Microsoft services such as Outlook.com, or have an Outlook 365 account at work. Otherwise, click the link to Sign up for a new account.

2. Let's get started offers you the choice of creating a new blank workbook, browsing the templates or accessing recent Excel files you may have stored on OneDrive, Microsoft's file storage service.

3. The Ribbon interface has fewer commands than the desktop version, but you can start your document online and then click OPEN IN EXCEL to send the document to your desktop version of Excel and carry on where you left off.

4. If you open a new workbook, you can rename it. Just click the default filename (something like 'Book 1') on the green title bar and rename it.

5. Whether you're working on a new spreadsheet or an existing one, Excel will automatically save your file – in fact, there is no Save command. It's easy to undo something, if you change your mind, by just pressing Ctrl + Z.

6. To edit the document, you have to be in Editing View rather than Reading View. Go to the View tab to change this.

7. Once in Editing View, you have all the basic spreadsheet features to enter data, add calculations, sort your data and even create charts.

8. Once finished, it's easy to share your document. Because it's stored online, you just send a link to your spreadsheet in OneDrive so others can work on it with you. Just press the Share button at the top of the page and fill in the details.

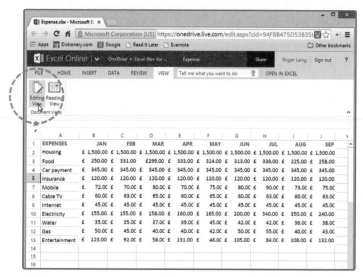

Above: To start making changes to your Excel file, make sure you are in Editing View.

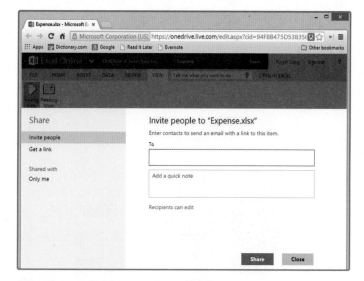

Above: Sharing sends a link to your online Excel file stored in OneDrive so others can work on it with you.

USEFUL WEBSITES AND FURTHER READING

WEBSITES

www.excelbanter.com
A forum that focuses only on Excel and
Excel-related topics.

www.exceltip.com
Tips on how to use Excel for data management,
calculations and other business-related tasks.
Also has Excel consultants and experts available to
answer questions.

www.mrexcel.com
Support and wide range of services for Excel.

www.office.microsoft.com/en-us/excel-help
Microsoft's official website for help and troubleshooting,
covering past and current versions of Excel.

www.ozgrid.com/Excel
A list of Excel formulas, plus tips and tricks
on how to use them.

FURTHER READING

Frye, Curtis D., *Microsoft Excel Step by Step*,
Microsoft Press, 2013

Harvey, G., *Excel 2013 All-in-one For Dummies*,
John Wiley & Sons, 2013

Jelen, B., *Microsoft Excel 2013 in Depth*, QUE, 2013

Lambert, Joan, *MOS 2013 Study Guide Microsoft
Excel*, Microsoft Press, 2013

MacDonald, M., *Excel 2013: The Missing Manual*,
O'Reilly Media, 2013

Murray, K., *Microsoft Office Professional 2013 Plain
and Simple*, Microsoft Press, 2013

Russo, M. & Ferrari, A., *Microsoft Excel 2013:
Building Data Models with PowerPivot* , Microsoft
Press, 2013

Schmuller, J., *Statistical Analysis with Excel
for Dummies*, John Wiley & Sons, 2013

Walkenback, J., *Excel VBA Programming
for Dummies*, John Wiley & Sons, 2013

Winston, W, *Microsoft Excel 2013: Data Analysis
and Business Modeling*, Microsoft Press, 2014

INDEX